THE GREEK TRAGEDY
IN NEW TRANSLATIONS

GENERAL EDITORS William Arrowsmith
and Herbert Golder

EURIPIDES: Iphigeneia at Aulis

EURIPIDES

Iphigeneia at Aulis

Translated by
W. S. MERWIN

and
GEORGE E. DIMOCK, JR.

OXFORD UNIVERSITY PRESS
New York   Oxford

OXFORD UNIVERSITY PRESS

Oxford   New York   Toronto
Delhi   Bombay   Calcutta   Madras   Karachi
Petaling Jaya   Singapore   Hong Kong   Tokyo
Nairobi   Dar es Salaam   Cape Town
Melbourne   Auckland

and associated companies in
Berlin   Ibadan

First published in 1978 by Oxford University Press, Inc.,
198 Madison Avenue, New York, New York 10016-4314
First issued as an Oxford University Press paperback, 1992
Oxford is a registered trademark of Oxford University Press

Library of Congress Cataloging-in-Publication Data
Euripides.
Iphigeneia at Aulis.
(The Greek tragedy in new translations)
I. Merwin, William S., 1927–
II. Dimock, George.   III. Title.
PA3975.17M4   1978   882'.01   76-51718
ISBN: 978-0-19-507709-4
20 19 18 17 16

Printed in the United States of America

EDITOR'S FOREWORD

The Greek Tragedy in New Translations is based on the conviction that poets like Aeschylus, Sophocles, and Euripides can only be properly rendered by translators who are themselves poets. Scholars may, it is true, produce useful and perceptive versions. But our most urgent present need is for a re-creation of these plays—as though they had been written, freshly and greatly, by masters fully at home in the English of our own times. Unless the translator is a poet, his original is likely to reach us in crippled form: deprived of the power and pertinence it must have if it is to speak to us of what is permanent in the Greek. But poetry is not enough; the translator must obviously know what he is doing, or he is bound to do it badly. Clearly, few contemporary poets possess enough Greek to undertake the complex and formidable task of transplanting a Greek play without also "colonializing" it or stripping it of its deep cultural difference, its remoteness from us. And that means depriving the play of that crucial otherness of Greek experience—a quality no less valuable to us than its closeness. Collaboration between scholar and poet is therefore the essential operating principle of the series. In fortunate cases scholar and poet co-exist; elsewhere we have teamed able poets and scholars in an effort to supply, through affinity and intimate collaboration, the necessary combination of skills.

An effort has been made to provide the general reader or student with first-rate critical introductions, clear expositions of translators' principles, commentary on difficult passages, ample stage directions, and glossaries of mythical and geographical terms encountered in the plays. Our purpose throughout has been to make the reading of the plays as vivid as possible. But our poets have constantly tried to remember that they were translating plays—plays meant to be produced, in language that actors could speak, naturally and with dignity. The poetry aims at being dramatic poetry and realizing itself in words and actions that are both speakable and playable.

Finally, the reader should perhaps be aware that no pains have been spared in order that the "minor" plays should be translated as carefully and brilliantly as the acknowledged masterpieces. For the Greek Tragedy in New Translations aims to be, in the fullest sense, new. If we need vigorous new poetic versions, we also need to see the plays with fresh eyes, to reassess the plays for ourselves, in terms of our own needs. This means translations that liberate us from the canons of an earlier age because the translators have recognized, and discovered, in often neglected works, the perceptions and wisdom that make these works ours and necessary to us.

A NOTE ON THE SERIES FORMAT

If only for the illusion of coherence, a series of thirty-three Greek plays requires a consistent format. Different translators, each with his individual voice, cannot possibly develop the sense of a single coherent style for each of the three tragedians; nor even the illusion that, despite their differences, the tragedians share a common set of conventions and a generic, or period, style. But they can at least share a common approach to orthography and a common vocabulary of conventions.

1. Spelling of Greek Names

Adherence to the old convention whereby Greek names were first Latinized before being housed in English is gradually disappearing. We are now clearly moving away from Latinization and toward precise transliteration. The break with tradition may be regrettable, but there is much to be said for hearing and seeing Greek names as though they were both Greek and new, instead of Roman or neoclassical importations. We cannot of course see them as wholly new. For better or worse certain names and myths are too deeply rooted in our literature and thought to be dislodged. To speak of "Helene" and "Hekabe" would be no less pedantic and absurd than to write "Aischylos" or "Platon" or "Thoukydides." There are of course borderline cases. "Jocasta" (as opposed to "Iokaste") is not a major mythical figure in her own right; her familiarity in her Latin form is a function of the fame of Sophocles' play as the tragedy par excellence. And as tourists we go to Delphi, not Delphoi. The precisely transliterated form may be pedantically "right," but the pedantry goes against the grain of cultural habit and actual usage.

As a general rule, we have therefore adopted a "mixed" orthography according to the principles suggested above. When a name has been firmly housed in English (admittedly the question of domestication is often moot), the traditional spelling has been kept. Otherwise names have been transliterated. Throughout the series the -os termination of masculine names has been adopted, and Greek diphthongs (as in Iphigeneia) have normally been retained. We cannot expect complete agreement from readers (or from translators, for that matter) about borderline cases. But we want at least to make the operative principle clear: to walk a narrow line between orthographical extremes in the hope of keeping what should not, if possible, be lost; and refreshing, in however tenuous a way, the specific sound and name-boundedness of Greek experience.

2. Stage directions

The ancient manuscripts of Greek plays do not supply stage directions (though the ancient commentators often provide information relevant to staging, delivery, "blocking," etc.). Hence stage directions must be inferred from words and situations and our knowledge of Greek theatrical conventions. At best this is a ticklish and uncertain procedure. But it is surely preferable that good stage directions should be provided by the translator than that the reader should be left to his own devices in visualizing action, gesture, and spectacle. Obviously the directions supplied should be both spare and defensible. Ancient tragedy was austere and "distanced" by means of masks, which means that the reader must not expect the detailed intimacy ("He shrugs and turns wearily away," "She speaks with deliberate slowness, as though to emphasize the point," etc.) which characterizes stage directions in modern naturalistic drama. Because Greek drama is highly rhetorical and stylized, the translator knows that his words must do the real work of inflection and nuance. Therefore every effort has been made to supply the visual and tonal sense required by a given scene and the reader's (or actor's) putative unfamiliarity with the ancient conventions.

3. *Numbering the lines.*

For the convenience of the reader who may wish to check the English against the Greek text or vice versa, the lines have been numbered according to both the Greek text and the translation. The lines of the English translation have been numbered in multiples of ten, and these numbers have been set in the right-hand margin. The (inclusive) Greek numeration will be found bracketed at the top of the page. The reader will doubtless note that in many plays the English lines outnumber the Greek, but he should not therefore conclude that the translator has been unduly prolix. In most cases the reason is simply that the translator has adopted the free-flowing norms of modern Anglo-American prosody, with its brief, breath- and emphasis-determined lines, and its habit of indicating cadence and caesuras by line length and setting rather than by conventional punctuation. Other translators have preferred four-beat or five-beat lines, and in these cases Greek and English numerations will tend to converge.

4. *Notes and Glossary*

In addition to the Introduction, each play has been supplemented by Notes (identified by the line numbers of the translation) and a Glossary. The Notes are meant to supply information which the translators deem important to the interpretation of a passage; they also afford the translator an opportunity to justify what he has done. The Glossary is intended to spare the reader the trouble of going elsewhere to look up mythical or geographical terms. The entries are not meant to be comprehensive; when a fuller explanation is needed, it will be found in the Notes.

ABOUT THE TRANSLATION

To the student of modern American poetry and the general reader, the name of W. S. Merwin needs no introduction. Now generally regarded as a major talent, he is also a proven trans-

lator who for years has earned most of his livelihood by translating from French (*The Song of Roland*; Chamfort's *Products of
the Perfected Civilization*), Spanish (*The Poem of the Cid*;
Lazarillo de Tormes), Portuguese, Latin (*The Satires of Per-
sius*), and Russian (*Osip Mandelstam, Selected Poems*). His
books of poetry include *A Mask for Janus* (1952); *The Dancing
Bears* (1954); *Green with Beasts* (1956); *The Drunk in the
Furnace* (1960); *The Moving Target* (1963); *The Lice* (1967);
The Carriers of Ladders (1970, and awarded the Pulitzer Prize);
and *The Compass Flower* (1977). He has also published two
volumes of short prose pieces, *The Miner's Pale Children*
(1970) and *Houses and Travellers* (1977).

Merwin's collaborator, George E. Dimock, is presently professor of Classics at Smith College. Awarded fellowships by both
the Guggenheim Foundation and the American Council of
Learned Societies, he is the author of numerous critical articles
on classical subjects and a forthcoming critical study of the
Odyssey.

Nowhere is scholarly timidity more evident than when the
scholar is dealing with a dubious text, its pages studded with
obelisks and emendations. And the corruption of the text of this
play, especially in the crucial finale, has meant, as Professor
Dimock points out, that the play has been treated with gingerly
and, at best, very lukewarm, enthusiasm. A pity, because even in
its mutilated shape the *Iphigeneia at Aulis* is clearly, with the
late *Orestes* and the posthumous *Bacchae*, one of Euripides'
most searching critiques of the malaise of Greek culture and
politics at the close of the fifth century. Because the play is a
critique of culture, still another of Euripides' great tragedies-of-
ideas, it is, I think, everywhere saturated in Homer, so haunted
by Homeric *arete* and echoes, and therefore concerned with the
contemporary perversion of that older arete. (For the same reason—revealing contrast—the Euripidean *Orestes* is haunted by
the *Oresteia*, and the *Bacchae*, I assume, by Aeschylus' lost *Bas-
sarids*.) Euripides wants his audience to see this event in epic
terms, to think and judge epically, at least at the outset; then,
later, when Agamemnon reveals himself for the slavish king he
really is—the kind of man who could kill his child to further his
own ambitions—we already have an epic standard of *arete* to
judge him by. Euripides, as so often, works here with systematic
anachronism; and anachronism works where there is a resonant

time, a coherent culture, which is constantly invoked; the contemporary application is increased, not diminished, by the epic contrast. We are compelled to see the action, or rather to resee it, in its own shockingly contrasting contemporary terms. Hence, I would argue, the leisurely, even lengthy, resonance of the Chorus with which the play begins, with its effective re-creation of the great roll call of Book II of the *Iliad*, the muster of all those heroic forces gathered against Troy under the leadership of the "king of men," Agamemnon. Then, in subsequent scenes, against this epic background, Euripides shows us the shabby reality, an Agamemnon who is literally enslaved to his own politics and the army which, after a lifetime of demagogic lying and irresponsible leadership, he has himself effectively corrupted.

The point is important. For this is a play, I think, whose most pervasive ramifying idea is the idea of "bad faith" (and its opposite, freedom and responsibility) exampled from the top. In the *Hecuba*, Euripides presents the Greek army as susceptible to compassion; it would, he suggests, respond affirmatively to moral suasion if its leaders had the courage to act morally, i.e., freely and responsibly. But in the *Iphigeneia at Aulis*—a much grimmer play on similar themes—the army is implacably opposed to the release of Iphigeneia. Why? Because, as Agamemnon tells Menelaos, "We are the slaves of the mob we lead." In sum, bad faith, *mauvaise foi*, in its full existential sense. But if so, this can only mean that Agamemnon and Menelaos have taught the army, their own men, *their* inhumanity (just as Odysseus, in Sophocles' great *Philoctetes*, corrupts the young Neoptolemos, who in turn corrupts his own crew). Euripides shows us, I am saying, Agamemnon and Menelaos in the act of creating the obscene necessity by which they are in fact mastered when they claim they would like to rebel against it. Bad faith, exampled from the top in a hierarchical society, is taught by a kind of downward contagion; and this corruption can, if practised long enough, turn into political "necessity." As it does here. Yet, at the same time, the obverse is true. Freedom too is taught by contagion. For when Agamemnon abruptly repents of his decision to sacrifice his daughter, Euripides shows us Menelaos suddenly changing too. For one brief, crucial moment there is the incredible sense that somebody here might act like a free agent at last, and we feel the explosive infection of this feeling. This, I think, not the dramatization of Agamemnon's vacillating character as portrayed by Homer, is the point. If Menelaos can be touched, then why not others, why not the army? *Arete*, like its opposite, can be taught—taught by the liberating contagion of example.

This infection of freedom is, to my mind, the major concern of the rest of the play. Why, we might begin by asking, does Euripides make Achilles such a priggish young man? Why does Achilles sound so callow, as though he had come to Aulis fresh from Professor Cheiron's lectures on sophistic ethics (compare the remarkably similar case of the young Pentheus in the *Bacchae*). Where, in short, is the great tragic Achilles of the *Iliad?* The answer lies, I believe, in Euripides' general strategy here, his dramatic deployment of his central theme, the contagiousness of freedom and/or bad faith. So far as I can see, there is only one person in this play who has an instinctive and passionate intuition of freedom; that person is, unmistakably, Iphigeneia. One may regret that she decides to offer her life in order that her barbarous and slavish father may prosecute his war against the Trojans. But in a play in which bad faith is persistently displayed by those who have the power to act, the importance of Iphigeneia's assertion of freedom, while under constraint, cannot be too strongly stressed. Her death may be futile (for what can be the end of a war led by such men as Agamemnon?), but this does not diminish the significance of the freedom she asserts. And *that* freedom, that responsibility, even that nobility (for generosity is, in Euripides, however naive, always noble), are essential not only to this corrupt society but to all human culture. Alcestis' free sacrifice of her life may be, given Admetos' character, naive; but it is, as the final epiphany of Alcestis as peer of Herakles and Orpheus shows, heroic, a free and responsible, a *noble*, confrontation with death. Whether Iphigeneia dies of her own free will or under constraint, the war against Troy will go on; for that war, pace Professor Dimock, she has no responsibility whatever. Her glory is that she alone asserts the hunger for freedom that is instinct in the species, until prevented by bad faith in those who govern or "lead," and especially visible in the young. In this respect she is simply the last in the long line of Euripides' self-sacrificing young people— but in the girls above all, for surely significant reasons—a line which begins with Alcestis, Makaria, Polyxena, and the others.

Like the others, she teaches the freedom and arete she embodies. If we ask, from this vantage point, why it is that Euripides makes his Achilles so priggish and callow, I think the answer is clear. In some real sense, the play enacts the heroic education of Achilles. From Cheiron he has learned the theoretical aspects of (sophistic) virtue; but his conduct everywhere betrays him. Is it then Euripides' purpose simply to show us an anti-heroic Achilles, for the sheer pleasure of "debunking"? If not, how can we divine in the young prig of this play the tragic hero of the *Iliad*, the greatest exemplar of the heroic code—*aien aristeuein?* He learns it—the idea of it, incarnated—from Iphigeneia who, though she has never been formally schooled, possesses in ample measure the instinctive passion and generosity of the young of the species. It may even be that she can exhibit what is native to her because she has not, like Achilles here, been corrupted by formal education and the male experience of political life. Euripides, in short, brings the experience of *his* play, *his* Iphigeneia, to bear upon the hero of the *Iliad*, just as he uses the *Iliad* itself to indict his contemporaries for their failure to evince the values, essentially Homeric, they still profess. Relentlessly the dramatist forces home the disparity between contemporary conduct and the epic ideal, while at the same time, out of the inhuman desert created by this latter-day Agamemnon, he shows us the old *arete* emerging, inchoate and naive, in the instinctive, untaught nobility of Iphigeneia, and then passing, by natural contagion, to the young man who will in turn, by the contagion of *his* example, teach it to the whole Greek world. The play dramatizes what has been lost, by juxtaposing memory with reality, then recreating the real as something not simply derived from an unrecapturable heroic past, but constantly recreated. *Arete*, in short, as innate and instinctive; the possession not of a class, or of men, or legendary heroes, but of the entire species, at any time, even now.

These remarks, I expect to be told, are at odds with the line taken by Professor Dimock in his Introduction. So much the better, it seems to me; where a classic is concerned, there should be disagreement. The peculiar peril of a classic is its liability to embalmment, its very capacity for using its greatness to intimidate its own readers, and thereby inevitably to erode its own greatness. Whatever value there may be in "scholarly consensus," there is no critical value in it whatever. Its effect upon the classic is to turn it into a huge, unchanging monolith of

Parnassian marble. The true classic, the so-called "inexhaustible" thing, is by definition never fully revealed; it is always waiting to disclose itself. Like Cézanne's wonderful array of Mont Sainte-Victoires, the sense of identical mountain-mass and scale is an illusion; the enduring rock changes constantly, with every hour, in every light and every season, with every alteration in vantage, weather, and perspective, endlessly disclosing itself as we, from our changing foreground, watch it or slowly revolve around it. Indeed, one of the virtues of any good translation, like the present one, is that it refuses to freeze or petrify the work, but encourages and requires constant variety of vision.

Baltimore, Maryland   William Arrowsmith

CONTENTS

IPHIGENEIA AT AULIS

INTRODUCTION

Euripides' *Iphigeneia at Aulis* was not produced until after the author's death, and it is generally thought to be, to some degree at least, unfinished. Many passages, particularly the end, are either unusually corrupted by time and interpolation, or did not receive the master's final touch, or both. Because the text is in this unsatisfactory state, it is natural that scholars should take the play as we have it less seriously than Euripides' other plays and should have dismissed as interpolations those parts of it which they did not like. They do this at their peril, however.

For one thing, Bernard Knox in an important article has effectively removed the only compelling grounds for suspecting major interpolations or serious incompleteness.[1] For another, the more we consider the manifest intent of the suspected passages, the more we seem to see not the banalities and cheap effects characteristic of interpolators, but the daring yet inevitable inventions of a writer who can be only Euripides. Who but Euripides could have ended this play with Clytemnestra denouncing the messenger's account of Iphigeneia's miraculous preservation? Clytemnestra considers that Agamemnon has fabricated it to forestall her wrath over her daughter's sacrifice, and no wonder, for we remember Agamemnon's lying tale which brought her to Aulis in the first place. Earlier in the play the Chorus has wondered whether such stories as that of Leda and

1. Bernard M. W. Knox, "Euripides' *Iphigenia in Aulide* 1-163 (in that order)," Yale Classical Studies 22 (1972).

the Swan have not been foisted on men "in the tablets of the
Muses," as though Euripides were preparing us specifically for
the doubt cast on the myth here. Thus the "happy" ending is
undercut in typically Euripidean fashion, even though this is
done in a suspected, obviously unmetrical passage. The truth
seems to be that the final page of the manuscript from which
our extant copies derive was not so much incomplete as partly
illegible,[2] and that even where our copies have not preserved
the exact language that Euripides wrote or would have written,
they have faithfully kept his conception. It is a brilliant one.

In Greek tragedy the figure of Iphigeneia embodies the question, "Why would anyone sacrifice his daughter's life as the
price of waging a punitive war?" And, thanks to Aeschylus' treatment of Iphigeneia in his *Agamemnon*, right behind that question stands another: "What sort of military victory is worth the
destruction of youth, of progeny, of the future of the race,
which such a war as the Trojan War brings upon both victors
and vanquished?" For Euripides the Trojan War was not worth
the life of even one girl; and by the same token neither was the
Peloponnesian War which Athens was losing even as Euripides
was writing this play. Yet, during the last twenty-five years of
Euripides' career, most of the Greek states had in fact been
sacrificing their youth and future to the Peloponnesian War,
just as in the myth Agamemnon showed himself willing to
sacrifice his daughter for the privilege of taking revenge on the
Trojans. We shall see that *Iphigeneia at Aulis* is Euripides' last
attempt to confront his fellow-Greeks with a picture of their
tragic folly.

So tragic in fact was the Peloponnesian War felt to be that
the great sophist Gorgias proposed a remedy for it in a famous
speech given at the Olympic games, probably in 408 B.C., two
years before Euripides' death.[3] The remedy, however, must have
seemed to Euripides worse than the disease: Gorgias recommended that the warring Greeks submerge their differences in a
common crusade against the "barbarian" Persians, a second
Trojan War as it were. Our play is among other things a response to this proposal of Gorgias', as its caricature of pro-

2. Sir Denys Page, *Actors' Interpolations in Greek Tragedy*, Oxford, 1934,
196.
3. Ulrich von Wilamowitz-Moellendorf, *Aristoteles und Athen* I, 172.
Berlin, 1893.

Hellenic, anti-barbarian chauvinism shows. In it Euripides makes clear to his fellow-Greeks how reasonable human beings, all of whom know better, consent to their own destruction in disastrous wars of aggression like the Trojan War, the Peloponnesian War, or the war against the Persians recommended by Gorgias. Doubtless, Euripides had lived too long and seen too much to hope that his play could prevent such insanity. Certainly his *Trojan Women* had not stopped the Athenian invasion of Sicily. But at least he could expose such adventures for what in his opinion they really were.

Iphigeneia at Aulis is a tragedy because it demonstrates inexorably how human character, with its itch to be admired (*philotimia* in Greek), combines with the malice of heaven to produce wars which no one in his right mind would want and which turn out to be utterly disastrous for everybody. In this play we shall see no tragic hero or heroine confronting some abyss in the universe, nor even a group of villains who do in the fair young maiden in spite of all her mother can do to prevent it; we simply shall see ordinary humanity acquiescing in its own destruction; but before we are finished we may agree with the author's evident feeling that few things can be more tragic than that.

As the play presents it, the situation is this: having got as far as Aulis on the east coast of Greece, the Greek expedition against Troy is held up for want of a wind. Kalchas the soothsayer has privately assured Agamemnon, Menelaos, and Odysseus that if Agamemnon will sacrifice his daughter Iphigeneia to the goddess Artemis, the winds will blow and Troy will be taken; if they do not, they will never reach Troy. Agamemnon has consented and has already sent for his daughter under the pretext of marrying her to Achilles, but as the play opens, he has had a change of heart. We see him, although he is still in a torment of indecision, send off a letter countermanding his instructions that Iphigeneia be brought to Aulis. In this way the conflict of the play is opened: whether or not it is worth even one human life to fight the Trojan War. At this stage nobody really doubts that the right thing to do is to save Iphigeneia. Agamemnon himself says, "What I have done / is wrong, and I want to undo it." In spite of his vacillation, he shows that he is as appalled at his previous actions as the old man who will bear his letter:

I have lost the use of my reason! My ruin
is straight ahead of me. No. Go. Start.
Run. Never mind the age in your legs.

From now on we experience the play as an agonizing effort to
save the life of Iphigeneia, an effort which turns out to be
doomed. Our horror mounts as we watch door after door close
upon her escape and, when finally she is led offstage to be sacrificed, even she now consenting to her own destruction, our dis-
may is complete.

Her ensuing miraculous "salvation" by the goddess, even if
we choose to believe in it, is no help at all. Clytemnestra has lost
her daughter as surely as though she had died; the only difference is that in this case she is not even allowed to mourn for
her (1953-8). And nothing has affected the demonstration that
perfectly "nice" people, when the moment comes, will sacrifice
children for the sake of military victory, no matter how unneces-
sary and damaging to the victors themselves such a victory
may be.

What makes the play especially devastating is that in the
beginning it seems, against all expectation, that Iphigeneia may
be saved. What could be more gratifying than to see even the
shameless politician Agamemnon come to the conclusion that
he cannot after all kill his own daughter? Then, to our delight,
in spite of his propensity to weakness and vacillation, he stands
firm against the importunities of his brother Menelaos, infatu-
ated with the idea of getting back Helen. When, after this,
Menelaos too comes round, we can scarcely contain our hope-
ful enthusiasm for Iphigeneia's salvation. It will be the reversal
of this tide of feeling, as Iphigeneia nevertheless comes to be
sacrificed, which will produce the play's peculiarly powerful
effect.

Gradually, inexorably, our hope is destroyed. Even after fate
has taken a hand and the letter has proved to be too late, even
after Iphigeneia has arrived and Agamemnon and Menelaos
have decided that there is no way to keep the common soldiers
from hearing about the oracle and compelling their leaders to
sacrifice the girl, there still seems to be a chance. Clytemnestra
has accompanied her daughter to Aulis. Surely she can think of
something? Admittedly before she discovers the truth we experience the almost unbearable scene in which Agamemnon,
while concealing it from his wife and daughter, makes it only

too plain to the audience that the proposed wedding means Iphigeneia's death; but will not Clytemnestra eventually find this out? She does find it out and she does think of something: she obtains an unconditional promise of protection from the man who is traditionally the greatest hero of them all, the supposedly incomparable Achilles. She and he concert a double plan: first, she and Iphigeneia are to plead with Agamemnon to see if he will not relent. If he does, an appeal to the army can at least be attempted. If he does not, or if the army is implacably set on the sacrifice, recourse can still be had to the supposedly invincible arms of Achilles.

As we might expect, the appeal to Agamemnon is a scene of extraordinary power. The women's case seems irresistible, and yet it fails. Agamemnon is sure that the army will kill him and the rest of his family and sacrifice Iphigeneia themselves if he fails to go through with the outrage. Pleading this compulsion, he goes offstage to make the final preparations for the ceremony himself.

It is at this point, really, that all is lost. Iphigeneia herself feels the trap closing, even though Achilles has not yet failed her, and sings a lament complaining of fate and the role of the gods. Apparently she has understood, as the audience soon will also, that only in legend can a hero, however great, prevail over a whole army by force. As if to make this point, Achilles enters to tell how the army has threatened to stone him to death. To be sure, he has brought his weapons and says that he is willing to undertake the battle in Iphigeneia's defense as he promised; but only a brief interrogation by Clytemnestra is needed to make it obvious that he cannot possibly succeed. It will be one man against thousands.

With the last door closed upon her escape, Iphigeneia decides to make a virtue of necessity, as Achilles indeed remarks afterwards. Her announcement of her decision begins as follows:

Mother, both of you, listen to me.
I see now that you are wrong
to be angry with your husband.
It is hard to hold out against the inevitable.

Accordingly she decides to die willingly "for Greece," and "with glory." Evidently a major part of her purpose is to prevent the loss of any more lives than her own, particularly the life of

Achilles; but in this of course, she will be unsuccessful. As the whole audience knows, he will be killed in the war. As she leaves the stage singing a hymn to Artemis in which she pictures herself as Troy's sacker and the preserver of the freedom of Hellas from barbarian rape, we are left desolate. If even under such circumstances as we have witnessed, Iphigeneia cannot be saved, and if youthful idealism such as hers can be made to accept, as it only too evidently can, such crude jingoism as her hymn implies, hope for mankind is dim indeed.

True, the play has often been read quite differently, as though Iphigeneia's unselfish adoption of her father's belated attempts to justify the war against Troy suddenly made it legitimate. But a closer look makes it hard to see how this can be. How can we forget what we so gladly welcomed in Agamemnon at the beginning of the play: his perception that it is wrong to kill his daughter in order to win a war over a worthless woman? He and his daughter have both submitted to the sacrifice on the assumption that it is a bowing to necessity, a poor second choice compared with what they know to be most desirable. What that is has seldom been put better than by Iphigeneia herself in her plea to her father:

. . . In three words I can say it all:
the sweetest thing
we ever see is this daylight. Under the ground
there is nothing.
Only the mad choose to be dead. The meanest life
is better than the most glorious death.

When all is lost and she chooses not to struggle for her life any longer or to imperil Achilles, Achilles unintentionally reveals to us what she is really doing:

. . . What you have said
is beautiful, and worthy
of your country. You are no match
for the gods, and you have given up
the struggle against them. You have reconciled
what should be with what must be.

The idea that Iphigeneia's sacrifice is inevitable is based first and foremost on the alleged lust for conquest of the mass of the Greek army. No doubt this lust is real enough once Agamemnon has spread abroad the oracle that Iphigeneia's sacrifice means certain victory. Without such encouragement, the army is obviously eager to go home because of the contrary winds at Aulis. According to Menelaos, "The Danaans / clamored for the ships to be sent home / and an end to these senseless efforts"; and Achilles speaks of the same feeling as persisting among his Myrmidons (1087-97) at the very time when, we realize, Agamemnon is arranging with Kalchas for his daughter's immolation (1015-18). Agamemnon publishes the oracle and arranges the sacrifice because he is sure Odysseus or Kalchas will do it if he doesn't (684-713), but how can he be sure? We have first seen him persuade Menelaos, its chief proponent, that the sacrifice is a crime against human nature: why can he not persuade Odysseus and Kalchas?* It is at least worth a try and, if that fails, even an attempt to persuade the army would be worth it. But Agamemnon is too much in the habit of bowing to what he assumes is the will of his constituency (29-31) to make any further effort to save his daughter; he ensures her death instead.

The rest is sheer excuse. Agamemnon had no difficulty in resisting the alleged obligation to Hellas as long as Menelaos was urging it (529-32); he pointed out that the gods had done his brother a favor in relieving him of a worthless wife (490-91). It is only some time after he feels his hand forced (720) that he says, "I owe it to Greece" (1019), and only for his daughter's benefit that he develops the finer flowers of his false patriotism. Indeed the speech in which he does this gives itself away. It begins with the truth, a vivid evocation of a war-crazed army, and manages only by the most violent illogic to end on a note of high-sounding morality:

. . . Look: how many ships,
the war fleet, assembled here, the proud men of Greece
and their bronze battle-gear, and they
cannot sail to the towers
of Ilion, and seize
the famous citadel, Troy,
according to Kalchas the prophet, unless I
sacrifice you.
Some strange Aphrodite has crazed
the whole Greek army with a passion to sail at once
to the barbarians' own country
and end this piracy of Greek marriage.
If I disobey the goddess, if I ignore
the oracle, then the army will sail to Argos,

* I thank the General Editor for this insight.

they will kill you and me, and your sisters
who are still at home. I have not become
Menelaos' creature. I am not guided by him.
It is *Greece* that compels me
to sacrifice you, whatever I wish.
We are in stronger hands than our own.
Greece must be free
if you and I can make her so. Being Greeks,
we must not be subject to barbarians
we must not let them carry off our wives.

The reference to Aphrodite in this speech by itself condemns
the expedition: what moral difference is there between the
Aphrodite who sent Paris to rape Helen out of Greece, and the
Aphrodite who is sending the Greeks to rape Troy? As for the
freedom of Greece,* what can it be worth when Greece's leaders are so evidently the slaves of what they take to be the pas-
sions of the mob? Finally, who are the real barbarians: the
Greeks who will sacrifice their own children, or the Trojans who
want to keep for themselves the most beautiful woman in the
world? As we suggested earlier, the last four lines of the speech
are nothing less than a patent caricature of Greek chauvinism.
These motives, which Iphigeneia innocently adopts, can never
convince us of the substantive value of her action, noble and
beautiful though we feel it to be.

Nowhere in Euripides, I think, is the conquest of Troy presented unequivocally as a good thing; in at least the great ma-
jority of instances it is a terrible example of man's inhumanity
to man, and our play is no exception. To be convinced of this
we have only to read what the Chorus sings at lines 1022-72, as
though to warn us against Agamemnon's "I owe it to Greece"
speech which I have just referred to. They describe the coming sack of Troy in terms completely sympathetic to the Trojans, and they are appalled at the destruction Helen will cause.
Later, having weighed the marriage of Peleus and Thetis and
the prediction that the fruit of it, Achilles, will destroy Troy
against Iphigeneia's coming death at the altar, they conclude
with the following question:

Oh where is the noble face
of modesty, or the strength of virtue, now
that blasphemy is in power
and men have put justice

* This and the following point I owe also to the General Editor.

behind them, and there is no law but lawlessness,
and none join in fear of the gods?

Even though they are Greeks, they see in the destruction of
Troy no justification for Iphigeneia's sacrifice, whether that
sacrifice is voluntary or not. When Iphigeneia does volunteer,
they praise her nobility, but add,

It is the role of destiny, in this,
and the role of the goddess,
that are sick.

Thus neither the content of Iphigeneia's patriotism, nor its
source, nor the Chorus's judgment of it, shows us anything in
which we may take comfort.

Most of all it is Iphigeneia herself who convinces us that her
gesture, for all its selfless nobility, is tragically mistaken. The
name of Helen echoes through the play as that of the one person most responsible for the horror we are witnessing, and we
are not surprised when Iphigeneia nobly refuses to play Helen's
role. In rejecting Achilles' offer to fight for her and consenting
to her own death, she gives the following as her ultimate justification:

I say what I am about to say
with no regard for anyone.
Tyndareos' daughter,
Helen, will bring on enough fighting, enough
death, for the sake of her body. As for you, stranger,
do not die for me,
and do not kill.
Let me save Greece if that is what I can do.

She wishes not to add to the bloodshed; but the terrible irony of
it all is that in consenting to the sacrifice she is consenting to
the whole Trojan War and the deaths of all the thousands who
will be killed in it. Achilles will be killing and dying on her
account at least as much as he will be killing and dying for
Helen, since without Iphigeneia's sacrifice neither he nor the
rest of the army can even sail to Troy, much less commit the
horrors the Chorus has been reminding us they will commit.

In the end Iphigeneia walks offstage to be sacrificed singing,

I who will conquer Troy
and bring down the city of Ilion.

In these lines Euripides forces us to identify her with Helen.
By the date of Euripides' play, the audience knew Aeschylus'
famous *Oresteia* practically by heart. In *Agamemnon*, the first
play of that trilogy, the Chorus sang (689) of the fatal name of
Helen, "death of ships, death of men, death of the city"—
helenas, helandros, heleptolis—and here in our play Iphigeneia
both calls herself *heleptolis* in the lines we quoted above and is
so called by the Chorus in its answer to her song. She has become as responsible as Helen for the expedition to Troy, for the
fall of the city, and for the miserable homecoming of the
Achaians.

She is, of course, though unwittingly, also responsible for Clytemnestra's murder of Agamemnon and Orestes' murder of Clytemnestra. In spite of what she thinks, she is hardly "bringing
salvation for Greece" (2004). In fact, the direct results of her
consenting to be sacrificed are worse than resistance would have
been. If, as Agamemnon feared, the army kills Achilles and the
Atreidai and sacrifices Iphigeneia against her will, at the least
there will be no matricide, and without Achilles to contend
with, Troy may well survive. All in all, it does not seem as
though we can regard Iphigeneia's noble gesture with satisfaction.

Nor is Artemis' alleged rescue of Iphigeneia in the play's
epilogue a sign of moral approval on the playwright's part. As
we have already noticed, it may be a hoax, and even if it is not,
it does nothing to mitigate either Clytemnestra's bereavement or
Agamemnon's and the Achaians' guilt. Kalchas' words hailing
the miracle, as reported by the messenger, demonstrate its moral
emptiness:

". . . Commanders
of the assembled armies of Greece, look:
the goddess has placed this victim
on her altar, a deer from the mountains,
and she accepts this instead of the girl,
rather than stain her altar with noble blood.
With this she is happy, and now she blesses
our voyage to attack Ilion."

Kalchas has not been presented in this play in such a way as
to inspire confidence in his interpretation of divine phenomena.
If, on the other hand, Artemis really "now . . . blesses this voyage to attack Ilion" as he says, we can only see the goddess as

corrupt; that is, if we regard the Trojan War in the light in which the Chorus and the goddess's own demand for Iphigeneia's sacrifice have taught us to regard it. In Aeschylus, Artemis demanded as the price of going to Troy that Agamemnon act out against his own progeny the destruction of the young which the war would bring. That at least was just and moral. Kalchas' Artemis by contrast refuses "to stain her altar with noble blood" at the very moment that she is "blessing" the voyage which will end in the death of Achilles and the decapitation of Priam, not to mention the destruction of the flower of Greece and the whole life of Troy.

Evidently Euripides included the rescue of Iphigeneia in his play partly at least in order to demonstrate its irrelevance from a moral point of view. He would be the more inclined to do so if it was, as seems likely, an original part of the story of Iphigeneia. The story may belong, like the story of Abraham and Isaac, to a type in which a divinity first demands the sacrifice of a human and then, for whatever reason, allows the substitution of an animal. Both Aeschylus in his *Oresteia* and Euripides in *Iphigeneia at Aulis* wanted to make a point not present in the original version, namely, the cruelty and callousness of a parent and an army who would sacrifice a child for the sake of military conquest. Aeschylus solved the problem of the substituted animal by omitting it and giving the impression that Iphigeneia was actually sacrificed, although it is interesting that not even he was completely unequivocal about this. Arrived in their narrative at the point where the knife must finally strike, Aeschylus' Chorus sings (*Agamemnon* 248-9, Lattimore),

What happened next I saw not, neither speak it.
The crafts of Kalchas fail not of outcome.

Theoretically even on this occasion Iphigeneia may have been saved. In *Iphigeneia at Aulis* on the contrary, Euripides has his messenger tell us specifically that the goddess substituted a deer for the girl; but, as we have already seen, this information is presented in a way and in a context which only deepen the negative implications of the sacrifice, indicting gods as well as men for the insanity of aggressive war.

In our play Euripides identifies the essential cause of aggressive war as *philotimia*, the urge to be thought superior (22, 342, 385, 520, 527 in the Greek text). Agamemnon even suggests

that prophets make predictions like the one concerning Iphigeneia because they "want only to be important," or, to put it
as the Greek has it, because they are *philotimon* (520). Though
startling at first, such an idea seems less surprising when we remember that at the beginning of the Peloponnesian War the
priests who managed the Oracle of Delphi had predicted victory
for the Peloponnesians "if they did their best."[4] Euripides, who
was no friend of the Oracle, evidently felt that that prediction
had done much both to encourage the outbreak of the war and
to raise Peloponnesian hopes once they were in it, thus making peace between Athens and Sparta more difficult. Such a feeling on Euripides' part would explain the assumption in the play
that it is the oracle that makes the army deaf to reason or pity
or longing for home. Under the circumstances it would be
natural for the poet to attribute the giving of such a response as
Delphi's to irresponsible self-importance. Whether or not the
Delphic institution believed that the prophecy itself was true, it
would manifestly have been better for Greece if it had been
suppressed. In like fashion the lust for war of the army in the
play is the more convincing when we recall the passion for victory which infected the Athenians and prevented peace on vari-
ous occasions during the Peloponnesian War. This too is *philotimia*. In fact, the measure of *philotimia*'s virulence is its uni-
versality. Iphigeneia's death at the altar, and thus the Trojan
War, is the work of the *philotimia* of everyone concerned.

In Agamemnon we see an individual in whom love of place
conquers his honesty in spite of his clear perception of the
counterfeit nature of rank and position. It is true that his better
feelings prevail briefly over his *philotimia*, but he seems almost
relieved to find his hand forced, and, unlike Clytemnestra, he
is only too proud and pleased at the thought that his daughter
has been taken away to dwell among the gods.

Menelaos is able to rise above his craving for Helen, but not
above his enjoyment of powerful connections. Agamemnon's
tears bring him over to his brother's side in the matter of saving
Iphigeneia, but when his brother changes back, he changes too.

Clytemnestra would clearly be willing to die for her child
many times over, but she is over-impressed with the social superiority of good form and Achilles' "greatness," indeed with

---

4. Thucydides, 2.54.

the whole aristocratic mystique. She consents too easily to the decorous restraints with which Achilles hobbles the defense of Iphigeneia, and she ought to know better than to submit so tamely to her daughter's misapplied patriotism.

Achilles in some ways is the most interesting case of all because he is an example of a whole theory of education whose goal is outlined by the Chorus (746-62). Everyone knows what is right, they sing, and training in humility and self-control can teach men to practice virtue. Achilles has been reared by the centaur Cheiron to protect him from the evil propensities of men (956-9), and if there is one thing he has learned, it is the ability to control himself by the use of reason (1266-72). In this, it is suggested, he is the opposite of Paris (763-79). We become aware almost instantly, however, that his education is vitiated by his sense of the importance of the heroic ideal and of himself as an epic hero. He vows magniloquently and often to save Iphigeneia's life, but entirely as a matter of honor, mostly his own, though he cares for hers as well. The one thing that his speeches do not contain is simple human feeling such as Paris might entertain: it does not seem to have occurred to him that a young girl is about to die. The epic *philotimia* of this most priggish young man ruins the effort to save Iphigeneia in at least four different ways. First, in the name of aristocratic decorum, he prevents Clytemnestra from making any of the emotional displays which might have moved the troops to pity. Second, out of social tact and not to risk his friendship with Agamemnon unnecessarily, he disassociates himself from the attempt to convince Agamemnon by argument. Third, when it finally becomes a question of his own action, he so lacks the common touch that he does not realize that the army will merely be infuriated and call him a slave to sex when he pleads that Iphigeneia is *his* bride (1800-10). Instead, he ought to try to convince them that no victory is worth what this one will cost. But that is not an idea which he himself could understand. He proclaims that for the sake of the expedition, he would have let Agamemnon use his name to trap Iphigeneia if Agamemnon had only asked him first (1321-31), and this is not the attitude of one who knows the value of human life. Fourth, his *philotimia* shows itself at perhaps its worst when, having bungled the defense of Iphigeneia in debate, he does not counsel flight but instead offers to defend her at the same time that he makes it

absolutely clear that thousands of men are coming to drag her
off by the hair. In that context, his pointing to his armor, his
vows to protect her and "stop Odysseus" are merely ludicrous.
No wonder Iphigeneia bows to the supposed inevitable. When
Achilles takes his leave, followed by his now demonstrably useless weapons, we are reminded of nothing so much as of Agamemnon's desertion of his daughter at the end of the previous
scene. Achilles will lay his arms near the altar, he says, in case
Iphigeneia should change her mind when the knife is at her
throat; yet how little he really expects to use those weapons is
shown by the sequel, in which not Agamemnon but he leads the
sacrificial procession and makes the prayer dedicating Iphigeneia to Artemis. The arms which were to protect her may be
lying close at hand, but the knife which will kill her, hidden
under the sacred barley in the basket, is the most important ob-
ject in the procession itself.[5] This Achilles, who makes not even
the mildest protest to Agamemnon and does nothing of any prac-
tical value to save the girl in spite of all his promises, is at most a
caricature of the Achilles of the *Iliad*. The generosity of Homer's
figure and his understanding of the meaning of death is not
there. Instead we feel that Euripides' Achilles is more than content that Iphigeneia should die—voluntarily, splendid creature!—and that he should live to go to Troy and wear the golden
armor of Hephaistos (1446-51). Our final image of him as he
leads the procession around the altar is not so much a picture
of treachery as of the impenetrability of heroic self-esteem.

Even Iphigeneia is infected with *philotimia*; she too has been
brought up under the heroic code. That is what induces even
her, who knew so well that the meanest life is better than the
most glorious death, to think of the tragic sacrifice which will
send the ships to Troy as her monument, her wedding, her children, the meaning of her life. Was innocence ever so abused?

There remain the Old Man and the Chorus. The Old Man
staunchly supports Clytemnestra, but it is clear that this is an
old retainer's proud loyalty to his original mistress rather than
recognition that the war is not worth it. He too has had his
speech to make in praise of "greatness" (32-7). The Chorus for
their part know that Agamemnon is wrong to sacrifice his daugh-

5. A brilliant discussion of this type of sacrifice and its connection with
tragedy is contained in Walter Burkert, "Greek Tragedy and Sacrificial
Ritual," *Greek, Roman, and Byzantine Studies* 7 (1966), 87-121.

ter, that "refusing to harm a child" is better. Contrasting Iphigeneia's sacrifice with the marriage of Peleus and Thetis, they are led to denounce the whole expedition against Troy as criminal. Yet even they have their passion for the men, the ships, and the armor, as we see in their entrance-song, and at the end, like everyone else, they "reconcile what should be with what [in their opinion] must be." The words with which they close the play are shocking:

Son of Atreus, sail
with a light heart to the land of Phrygia,
and return with a light heart
and heavy spoils
from Troy.

Their worst lapse, however, occurs at the moment of Clytemnestra's and Iphigeneia's arrival in the camp. The Chorus knows what is in store for Iphigeneia but, warned to keep silent by Agamemnon, they do not tell. Under the circumstances their concern not to frighten the tender "bride" is grisly.

The Chorus in fact affects us as though it had a peculiar kind of double vision. Its instincts in general are good; it knows what is right, but at the same time it knows what is supposed to happen, and that deprives its good words of much of their force. It has heard of the prophecy made at Peleus'. marriage that Achilles would win glory at Troy (1440-52), and therefore even as it begs Agamemnon to listen to his wife's plea or applauds Achilles' promise to save Iphigeneia's life, it must feel fairly sure that there is no hope. When at the end of the play its hopelessness is not only proved correct, but apparently given heaven's seal of approval, it is not surprising that the Chorus too lapses into the old *philotimia* and "reconciles what should be with what must be."

This idea of "what must be" is contributed to by the "destiny" and the "role of the goddess" which the Chorus finds "sick" (1897-9). Iphigeneia makes her own comment on this sort of destiny when, after she has traced her own fate all the way back to Hecuba's dream and the "Judgment of Paris," she sings of the winds of Zeus which bring happiness to some and despair to others (1716-68). Why must the winds which will bear the fleet to Troy involve her death? It is all so arbitrary. Can this really be the "what must be" with which "what should be" must be reconciled? If this were all, our world would be dark indeed; but actually Euripides' play offers us an escape from the clutches of philotimia and fate.

The Chorus's belief in the prophecy of Achilles' future, like Iphigeneia's belief in the prophecy of Paris' future, suggests how philotimia and belief in destiny are related. Both are rooted in acceptance of the truth of the Greek myths. In them "greatness," that is, the world's regard, is what men desire above all, and it is won almost exclusively by military success. Military success, in turn, is administered arbitrarily by fate and the gods. In other words, it is tragic. This state of affairs leaves men nothing to do but to fight and accept their fate. The struggle for military superiority is everything, and realizing this we can better understand the war-madness of the rank and file of the army in the play. On the assumptions of the myths, philotimia is the only alternative. As for belief in fate, it is for obvious reasons peculiarly a soldier's attitude, and the myths reinforce the tendency to entertain it. In the old tales, the end is always known, and the habit which this inculcates of looking for the fulfillment of a known outcome encourages regarding any human situation as one whose issue is determined by fate and the gods. This known outcome is the "what must be" against which the characters in the myths struggle in vain, just as Iphigeneia and the Chorus do in our play.

But what if the old tales are not true, as our play has at least suggested? Then greatness may not be all in all for men, and no end is necessarily inevitable. Necessity, destiny, the gods even, may not exist and need not be served. By questioning the myths our play potentially destroys the basis both for philotimia and for belief in destiny.

Even when the myths are largely accepted, Iphigeneia at Aulis shows us that their influence can be resisted. It shows us how even in such indifferently endowed characters as Agamemnon and Menelaos, brought up though they have been to the heroic way of life, human feeling can prevail over the mystique of greatness, at least for a while. Furthermore, when they succumb, they succumb to a presumed political necessity rather than to the mythological one. It is true that the political necessity is the result of the army's acceptance of the values and world-view of the myths, but we now see that that view, some day perhaps can be overcome: if, for example, enough people ponder deeply plays like this one.

In *Iphigeneia at Aulis* Agamemnon and Menelaos encourage us to resist not only the supremacy of *philotimia*, but the idea of mythological necessity as well. They do this by casting doubts on the skill of prophets and the efficacy of prophecy. Their strictures against Kalchas cause us, observing the fact that he is the lone authority for the demands of Artemis, to be filled with questions like, Why believe Kalchas? Who knows whether Iphigeneia's death will make the wind blow? Why does not someone ask the Greeks these questions in the effort to save her? Such questioning on the part of the play's audience can only make it less willing to accept the authority in the play of the mythological ideas of "what must be" and of *philotimia* alike.

More than all this, the play encourages us to fight against what seems necessity in the most drastic way of all, absolutely, even without hope. It does this by making us recoil so violently at the spectacle of a man giving in to necessity in so extreme a situation: a father deliberately arranging to have his daughter's throat cut. Most of us, less subject to *philotimia* than Agamemnon, would risk our own deaths and those of our whole family before we would in person arrange for the sacrifice of our child. Again, questions crowd upon us: What would have happened if Agamemnon and Menelaos, even without hope, had undertaken to win Odysseus' and Kalchas' silence by force or persuasion? Or, when that failed, what if they had made supplication together with Clytemnestra and the children before the whole army? What if they had fled to Mycenae with what followers they could muster and had attempted to defend "the walls the Cyclopes built?" The play demands that we ask these questions by its very emphasis on the fact that these things were *not* done. Clytemnestra and Iphigeneia failed to supplicate Achilles in public before the army, and Clytemnestra failed to seek Achilles through the host, all from a false sense of decorum and *noblesse oblige*. What would have happened if they had? Or, finally, what would have happened if Iphigeneia had let Achilles fight for her, and Clytemnestra had clung to her daughter and made Odysseus drag her off by the hair? At the very least there would have been the satisfaction of not submitting tamely to a personal outrage; nor would Iphigeneia and her mother have been led to accept the false and in this play's terms degrading notion that the Trojan War was a patriotic duty for all Greeks. Let us suppose that none of these things would have been enough to save Iphigeneia, and that any or all of them might have caused the deaths of Agamemnon, Menelaos, Clytemnestra, Orestes, and Agamemnon's other daughters into the bargain. Even so, it would have been both a more edifying human spectacle and less destructive in the end. And if others should be led by such an example to refuse in the same way to play the game of heroic superiority, who would say that the tyranny of tragic Necessity might not in time be broken?

Best of all, we can see that *Iphigeneia at Aulis* shows us how to be free of necessity not just in the distant future but at any time, and that this was a demonstration of which the contemporary audience stood in desperate need. In the play Agamemnon has said, in effect, "I must kill you, my dear daughter, for if I do not, we shall all die and our country will lose its freedom." In Euripides' last years precisely the same argument was undoubtedly being used to persuade the citizens of Athens to continue their by then hopeless war against the Peloponnesians. Looking at the play in the way we have been doing, we can see that through it Euripides was saying to the Athenians something like the following:

You fear for your freedom. What slavery could be so terrible as the things this war is forcing you to do? You are already slaves many times over. You fear for your lives; yet like Iphigeneia you are willing to sacrifice yourselves, or like Agamemnon to sacrifice your children, in order to fight a war you cannot win. Why will you not instead, by making peace, by surrendering even, risk your lives and your freedom for the sake of peace? Even if it should mean the end of Athens, as it almost surely will not, there will be other men, other cities, and Athens, instead of destroying herself body and soul as she is now doing, will be remembered by men of understanding as a city which came to an end more noble than even Iphigeneia's. For those who know when and how and for what to die, "necessity" holds no terrors.

Athens surrendered in 404 B.C., two years after Euripides' death and not until she had lost her last fleet and suffered the starvation attendant on a four months' siege. As we suggested at the beginning, even so eloquent a play as *Iphigeneia at Aulis* does not stop wars by itself. Yet in the end the Athenians did give evidence that they had understood what Euripides was saying. One of the terms of the surrender, when it came, was that the Athenians should destroy that part of their walls on which their power at sea depended. Xenophon tells us that they did so (*Hellenica* 2.2.23),

to the music of flute girls and with great rejoicing, for they considered that that day was the beginning of freedom for Greece.

Evidently Euripides was not the only Athenian happy to turn his back on *philotimia* and surrender his city's dominance in exchange for a more equitable and equable world.

Northampton   :ORGE E. DIMOCK, JR.

IPHIGENEIA AT AULIS

CHARACTERS

AGAMEMNON King of Mycenae, leader of the Greek
expedition against Troy

OLD MAN Clytemnestra's slave, attendant on Agamemnon

CHORUS of young women of Chalkis

MENELAOS brother of Agamemnon, husband of Helen of Troy

FIRST
MESSENGER leader of Clytemnestra's escort

SUPERNUMERARY
CHORUS of Clytemnestra's attendants

CLYTEMNESTRA Queen of Mycenae

IPHIGENEIA daughter of Agamemnon and Clytemnestra

ORESTES infant son of Agamemnon and Clytemnestra

ACHILLES hero-to-be of the Trojan War

SECOND
MESSENGER

Scene: In front of Agamemnon's tent, in the camp of the Greek armies by the bay at Aulis, where the ships are waiting. It is some time before dawn. As the light rises it will be perceived that the tent has a main entrance flanked by two side doors. AGAMEMNON *enters through the main door, a waxed tablet in his hand. He paces up and down before the tent in great indecision, then turns and calls in at the main door.*

AGAMEMNON Come here, old man. In front of my tent.

OLD MAN (*inside*) I'm coming. Is there something new,
        King Agamemnon?

AGAMEMNON Be quick about it!

OLD MAN (*entering*) I am quick. There's no sleep in me.
        My eyes won't stay shut now they're old.

AGAMEMNON What star is that, what time
        crossing heaven?

OLD MAN Sirius, pursuing the seven Pleiades,
        still traveling high at this hour.

AGAMEMNON No bird-sound, no murmur from the sea.
        The winds are silent along these
        straits of Euripos.

OLD MAN Then why are you up
        pacing outside your tent, King Agamemnon?
        There's not a voice stirring yet in Aulis.
        The watch is quiet
        up on the walls.
        Might we not go in?

AGAMEMNON I envy you, old man. I envy any man
        whose life passes quietly, unnoticed by fame.
        I do not envy those in authority.

OLD MAN But it is they who have the good of life.

AGAMEMNON You call that good? It's a trap. Great honors
taste sweet
but they come bringing pain.
Something goes wrong
between a man and the gods
and his whole life is overturned.
At other times the notions of men, all
different and all insatiable,   30
grate it away by themselves.

OLD MAN I don't like it, hearing a king
talk that way. Atreus did not
sire you, Agamemnon, into a world
of pure happiness. You must expect
to suffer as well as rejoice,
since you're a man.
And the gods will see to that, whether
you like it or not.
But you've lit your lamp. You've written   40
some message. That's what you have in your hand.
You keep putting on
the seal and taking it off again.
You write and then you
rub out what you've written.
You drop it to the ground, and tears
stream down your face.
From what I can see
despair appears to be driving you
out of your reason. Oh my king,   50
Agamemnon, tell me what it is.
I am a man of good will, I am
loyal to you, you can trust me with it.
I was in your
wedding procession, don't you remember,
back at the start. Tyndareos gave me
to your wife as part of the dowry,
because I could be trusted.

AGAMEMNON Leda, the daughter of Thestios, had three
girls of her own: 60
Phoibe, and my wife Clytemnestra,
and Helen.
And the highest-born young men in Greece came
asking to marry
Helen.
And threatened each other,
looking for blood. Each of them said
that if he himself did not get to marry her
he would murder whoever did.
So her father Tyndareos   70
could not think what he should do to avoid disaster.
Should he give her to one of them
or not let her marry at all?
Then he thought of a way.
The suitors would have to take an oath, all of them
together, a solemn oath, sealed
with a burnt offering,
swearing to defend whichever of them
should win Helen, Tyndareos' daughter, for his wife.
And if anyone   80
should ever carry her off, and keep
her husband from her bed, whether
he came from Greece or somewhere else, they would all
make war on his city and bring it to the ground.
So they swore. Old Tyndareos
was sharper than they were:
when it was over he left the choice to his daughter.
He said, "Now why shouldn't she marry
as the sweet breath of Aphrodite directs her?"
And her love fell—that's the pity of it—   90
on Menelaos.
It was later
that this Paris, who judged
the beauty of goddesses,
as the Argives tell it,
came from Phrygia to Sparta. There were gold flowers
stitched onto his clothes,

27

he glittered with barbarian jewels,
he loved her.
She returned it. While Menelaos was away 100
he carried her off with him
to the summer pastures of Ida.
Menelaos, stung by his fate, raged
through all Greece, reminding
everyone who had sworn that oath
that they were bound to come to his help now.
And the Greeks rushed to arms. And they have come
to the straits of Aulis
with their fighting gear, their ships, their shields,
their chariots, their horses. 110
And because Menelaos is my brother, they chose
me to be their general.
I wish they had saved the honor for someone else.
And when the whole army had mustered
here at Aulis,
the wind died. Calm. We still cannot sail.
There is only one hope of our going,
according to Kalchas,
the prophet. Iphigeneia, my daughter,
must be sacrificed to Artemis, 120
the deity of this place.
Then the wind will take us to Troy,
and the city will fall to us.
When I heard this I called Talthybios the herald
and said, "Sound the trumpet, sound it,
and tell them all to go home. I could never
make myself kill my own daughter."
But at that my brother started reasoning with me,
arguing, urging me
to commit this horror, 130
till I wrote a letter telling my wife
to send our daughter here
to be married to Achilles.
I told her
what a great man he is, and I said

    he would not sail with us until a bride
    from our own family
    had been sent to his home in Phthia.
    A story I made up
    so that my wife would send the girl.   140
    Among the Achaians the only ones who know
    are Kalchas, Odysseus, and Menelaos.
    And what I have done
    is wrong, and I want to undo it. That is why
    I wrote this second letter that you found me
    sealing and unsealing. Take it. Go to Argos.
    I will tell you what it says
    since you are loyal to my wife and my house. (*Reads.*)
    "Clytemnestra, daughter of Leda,
    I mean this letter to rule out the first one." (*Pauses.*)   150

OLD MAN   Tell me the rest. Read it. Then I will be able
          to repeat the message myself
          as it is in the letter.

AGAMEMNON   (reads) "Do not send your daughter
            to this folded harbor of Euboia,
            Aulis,
            a shore where no waves come in.
            We will find some other time for her marriage."

OLD MAN   But Achilles, when he learns
          there's no bride for him after all,   160
          will he not blaze up
          raging against you and your wife? That
          frightens me. How will you deal with that?

AGAMEMNON   Only his name has been used. Achilles himself
            knows nothing
            of our plans, the marriage,
            what I said about giving him my daughter
            as his bride.

OLD MAN Then you promised her to the son of a goddess
simply to fetch her here   170
to be a victim for the Argives! King Agamemnon,
your daring appalls me.

AGAMEMNON I have lost the use of my reason! My ruin
is straight ahead of me. No. Go. Start.
Run. Never mind the age in your legs.

OLD MAN I will lose no time, my lord.

AGAMEMNON Do not pause at the springs in the shade,
nor stop to sleep.

OLD MAN The gods keep me from it!

AGAMEMNON When you get to where roads fork, take a sharp look   180
down all of them. Make sure
no chariot slips past you,
too fast or not noticed,
bringing my daughter here to the Greek ships.

OLD MAN It shall be done.

AGAMEMNON If she has left the palace
and you meet her and her escort
make them turn back. Take
the reins yourself and shake them loose
and urge on the horses to Mycenae   190
where the Cyclopes built the walls.

OLD MAN One thing. What will make your wife
and your daughter trust me
when I tell them the message?

AGAMEMNON This seal, on the letter.
Take it, and go now. Day
is breaking. Already the sun's

chariot of fire has sent
brightness into the sky. Go. Take up
your task. We must all suffer.   200

The OLD MAN *goes off right.*

No mortal
ever knows happiness and good fortune all
the way to the end.
Each one is born with his bitterness waiting for him.

He goes in through the main door. The CHORUS *of young
Chalkidian women enters left.*

CHORUS I have crossed the narrows
        of Euripos, I came sailing and I beached
        at Aulis, on the sands. I left
        Chalkis, my city, where the spring
        of Arethousa wells up and runs flashing
        down to the sea. I came   210
        to see for myself this army of the Achaians,
        the oar-winged ships of the heroes,
        the thousand galleys
        which blond Menelaos and Agamemnon of the same
        great lineage sent,
        as our husbands tell us,
        to fetch Helen again:
        Helen.
        Whom Paris the herdsman seized
        from the reedy bank of the river Eurotas   220
        where Aphrodite had led her for him, after
        the goddess had bathed in the dewy fountain
        and taken her place beside
        Hera and Pallas Athene
        for her beauty to be judged.
        Through the grove
        where the victims die on the altar
        of Artemis I came

running, and I blushed for shyness
at my fever to see   230
the pitched strength of the Danaans, the tents
hung with weapons, the clanging
press of armed horsemen.
Now I set eyes
on the two that are named Aias, I see
Oïleus' son and that son of Telamon
who is the hope of Salamis,
and with them Protesilaos,
and Palamedes, child of Poseidon's son,
hunched down, weaving   240
their cunning into a game of draughts.
Near them is Diomedes
delighting in throwing the discus,
and Meriones, scion of Ares,
wonder of men. Laërtes' son
has come there from his craggy island,
and Nireus, most handsome of the Achaians.
I have seen wind-footed Achilles
in full armor racing over the sands:
Thetis' son, whom Cheiron reared,   250
and he was racing against horses,
four of them, and a chariot, on the curved track.
I saw the beauty of those horses, gold
worked into their bits and bridles,
the yoke pair dappled
gray with white in their manes, the trace horses
bays with dappled white fetlocks;
and Eumelos, the grandson of Pheres,
driving them, shouting,
goading them on faster, and they   260
hugged the turns, but Peleus' son
in all his armor stayed with them the whole way,
never falling behind the chariot rail and the axle,
and won.
And I came to where the ships lie. Even a god
would find no words for the way that sight

stirs a woman's eyes. Pleasure took my breath away.
The fleet of the Myrmidons from Phthia, fifty
lean vessels, lay to the right
bearing statues   270
of the sea-god's daughters, the Nereïds, in gold,
high on their sterns,
to show that those ships were Achilles'.
Next to them lay the galleys of the Argives,
their admiral
Mekisteus' son, whom Talaos
brought up to manhood;
and Sthenelos, Kapaneus' son, was there.
Then the sixty ships from Attica; the son
of Theseus is their commander, and their ensign   280
is Pallas Athene with her winged chariot
and its horses, a sign which lightens the hearts
of mariners.
Then the flotilla of fifty ships
from Boiotia with their ensign rising
from each of the sterns: Kadmos
holding a dragon of gold. Leïtos,
born of the earth,
is their admiral. And the same number
of ships from Lokris, commanded by the son   290
of Oïleus, who had come
from the famous city of Thronion
to moor beside them.
The son of Atreus had brought a hundred vessels
from Mycenae
where the Cyclopes built the walls. The king
his brother and companion-in-command,
sailed with him to bring vengeance
on the bride who had abandoned his house
to lie with a barbarian. I saw the ships   300
from Pylos, that Gerenian Nestor brought,
and their sign is the river
Alpheios, that flows
by his country, shown on his sterns

in the form of a bull. Then the twelve
Ainian vessels that obey King Gouneus,
and near them the lords of Elis, who are called
the Epeians: Eurytos commands
the ships that came with them.
And the white-oared Taphian galleys followed   310
King Meges, Phyleus' son, from the rocky islands
of Echinai that frighten sailors.
To the left
the twelve sleek galleys of Aias of Salamis
made up the end of the line
that ran back down the beach
without a break, beside the army. The barbarian
who joins battle with these should not
cling to his hopes of sailing home.
I have seen the whole fleet,   320
and when it is famous and they
tell of it where I live
I will remember.

          MENELAOS and the OLD MAN enter right, quarreling.

OLD MAN Menelaos, you have no right to do this!

MENELAOS Get away! You are too loyal to your master.

OLD MAN Your reproach does me honor.

MENELAOS You'll be sorry if you go on meddling.

OLD MAN You had no right
         to open the letter I was carrying.

MENELAOS And you had no right to carry a letter   330
          that would harm the Greek cause.

OLD MAN Argue with others about that.
         Give me the letter.

MENELAOS I will not.

OLD MAN (*seizes him*) Then I won't let go.

MENELAOS I'll bloody your head with my scepter.

OLD MAN What greater glory than to die for my master?

MENELAOS Let go! Your words are too big for a slave.

OLD MAN (*calling in at the main door of the tent*) Master! Help!
                                            This man
      snatched your letter out of my hand,   340
      Agamemnon! Mutiny!

                 AGAMEMNON *enters from the main door.*

AGAMEMNON What is this? Brawling and arguing
      outside my tent door?

MENELAOS My voice takes precedence here, I believe.
      At a sign from AGAMEMNON, *the* OLD MAN *goes in at the*
                             right-hand side door.*

AGAMEMNON How did you come to quarrel
      with this old man, Menelaos?
      And why were you so violent with him?

MENELAOS Look at me, Agamemnon. Then I will
      start to tell you.
AGAMEMNON Do you think I'm afraid   350
      to look you in the eye, Menelaos?
      I am a son of Atreus.

MENELAOS Do you see this letter? It was meant
      to betray all of us.

AGAMEMNON That letter—in the first place
      give it back to me.

35

MENELAOS Not until I have told the Greeks what it says.

AGAMEMNON You mean you broke the seal. So you know
what you have no business knowing.

MENELAOS Yes I broke the seal. And it's you   360
who will suffer as a result, for acting
behind our backs.

AGAMEMNON How did you come to find him? Oh gods
what shamelessness!

MENELAOS I was watching for the arrival
of your daughter from Argos.

AGAMEMNON You see? Shameless again! What right have you
to spy on what concerns me?

MENELAOS I chose to. I'm not your slave.

AGAMEMNON This is beyond endurance! Am I not to be allowed   370
to govern in my own house?

MENELAOS No, because you're not to be trusted.
You never were, you aren't to be trusted now,
you never will be.

AGAMEMNON How smooth you are with your slanders.
I despise a nimble tongue.

MENELAOS How do you feel about a mind
true to nothing and no one? It is you
who must answer for yourself. And don't try
to shout down the truth   380
just because you're angry.
I won't be too harsh with you.
Have you forgotten the fever
of your ambition at the first thought

36

of leading an army against Troy?
You pretended
not to want the command but really
you'd have paid anything to be general.
You know how you humbled yourself
at the time. Touching hands,   390
keeping open house to the whole
citizenry,
making them all speak to you, one by one,
whether they wanted to or not.
Anything
to entice preferment out of the crowd.
But once you'd been chosen to command, all that changed.
You dropped the friends you didn't need any more.
It was hard to get to talk with you, you shut
yourself in.   400
Is one to admire a man
who changes as soon as he gets what he wants
and turns from friends
the moment he's in a position to help them?
That's the first point
in which I found you wanting, Agamemnon.
Next, you led the combined armies
of the Hellenes here to Aulis
and then at one stroke all your importance
collapsed   410
just because the wind fell.
You were nothing
if the gods would not fill your sails. And the Danaans
clamored for the ships to be sent home
and an end to these senseless efforts.
I haven't forgotten the sight
of your face when you heard that. What anguish,
what gloom at the thought
that you might not sail in, after all,
lord   420
of a thousand ships
flooding Priam's beach with arms. Then you asked me

to help you. "What shall I do? Isn't there
something I can do?" Anything
rather than lose the command
and the glory.
Then when Kalchas said, "Yes:
sacrifice your daughter to Artemis
and the Greek ships
will be able to sail,"   430
how happy you were to promise.
And no one—admit it—forced you
to write to your wife
and tell her to send the girl here,
pretending that she would marry Achilles.
Then you change your mind,
you unburden yourself of a different message
and it's discovered.
At this point you'd never murder your daughter.
Well. This same sky   440
watched you speak otherwise. It's true
men find this happening to them
all the time. They sweat and clamber
for power until it's theirs,
then all at once they
fall back and amount to nothing again.
Sometimes it's the fault of the populace,
too stupid to know who's talking sense.
Other times it's richly deserved: the leaders
turn out not to be able   450
to keep the city safe.
I grieve above all
for Greece and her mortification.
She had set her heart on glory. Now
she will have nothing to answer
when the barbarian trash laugh at her,
thanks to you and your daughter.
Oh I would never put a man at the head
of a country or an army
just because of his connections.   460
A general needs to have a mind.

CHORUS It is terrible when discord
        divides brothers
        and they fight each other with words.

AGAMEMNON It's my turn now. And I'll keep my
           reproach dignified: brief,
           restrained.
           Not staring wide, shamelessly, but with
           modesty, remembering that you
           are my brother. No man who amounts to anything   470
           is without a sense of shame. You
           come to me in a passion,
           breathing hard, eyes
           suffused with blood. Tell me, who
           has wronged you? What do you want? Are you pining
           for a virtuous wife? I'm afraid
           I can't do much for you there. The one you had
           is no credit to your government.
           Am I, then, supposed to suffer
           for your shortcomings   480
           when they're no fault of mine? It's not
           my ambition that is biting you.
           You care about nothing,
           nothing but holding a beautiful woman in your arms.
           You've abandoned all decency, all sense.
           The passions of a degraded man are degraded.
           And if I was mistaken to start with, and later
           was wise enough to change my mind,
           is that madness? No, you're the one who's mad.
           The gods in their kindness took a bad wife off your
                                                       hands   490
           and you're trying to get her back.
           The suitors, it's true,
           were so misguided
           as to swear an oath to Tyndareos
           while the lust was on them. In my view
           some goddess—Hope, I imagine—accomplished that.
           Not you in any case.
           Still, lead them, by all means

39

to fight your war for you. They're foolish enough
to stick to their oaths. But the gods   500
will not be fooled. They can recognize
oaths that were set up as traps, and sworn to
under duress.
I will not kill my children.
There's no justice in things turning out
precisely the way you want them to—you get
your vengeance on a worthless wife—
while my days and nights melt
in tears, at the unholy
crimes I've committed against my own children.   510
These are the few things
I wanted to say to you once and for all.
You should be able to understand them.
You can refuse
to be sensible if you want to. But for my part
I will set straight my own affairs.

CHORUS   This is not what was said before.
         But the change
         is for the better:
         refusing to harm a child.   520

MENELAOS   Oh misery! Then I see I have no friends.

AGAMEMNON   When you have friends you try to destroy them.

MENELAOS   Is there no way that you will show
           that you are my father's son?

AGAMEMNON   I will share your reason, not your madness.

MENELAOS   You would share my troubles, if you were a brother and
                                                        a friend.

AGAMEMNON   Say that when you have behaved like a brother and a
                                                     friend to me,
           not when you are doing me harm.

MENELAOS And Greece—you mean you'll abandon her now
          to her struggle?   530

AGAMEMNON Greece has been driven mad by the same god
           who drove you out of your senses.

MENELAOS Congratulate yourself on your scepter
          now that you've betrayed your own brother.
          I'll find some other way, other friends—

                              Enter a MESSENGER *right.*

MESSENGER Commander of all the armies of Greece, King
           Agamemnon, I have brought you,
           from home, your daughter
           whom you called Iphigeneia.
           And her mother, your Clytemnestra, is with her,   540
           and the boy Orestes. You've been away from home
           a long time, and the sight of them
           will be a joy to you.
           It's been a tiring journey, and they are resting
           now, bathing their soft feet
           at the flowing spring,
           and the horses are resting too;
           we turned them loose to graze there in the good pasture.
           I came on ahead to tell you,
           so that you would be ready. But rumor   550
           travels faster. The army knows
           your daughter is here. And they are running
           and crowding to get a look at the girl;
           everyone wants to catch a glimpse
           of those whom fortune has blessed.
           They say, "Is there going to be a wedding,
           or did King Agamemnon miss the child
           so much that he sent for her?" Others say,
           "Offerings are being made
           consecrating the child to Artemis,   560
           goddess of Aulis,

41

as though for a wedding, but who
will be the bridegroom?" Come. Do
what comes next, Agamemnon. Bring the sacrificial
basket, and lead the procession
around the altar. Set the garlands on your heads.
King Menelaos, prepare
the marriage feast. Let the flute
trill within doors and the floor
resound with the dancing, for this is the day   570
that dawned to see your child made happy.

AGAMEMNON Thank you. You may go inside. What is left to do
no doubt will turn out well, in the course of fate.

                    The MESSENGER *goes in at the right-hand door*
Oh miserable creature that I am,
now what can I say? Where
can I begin in the face of this misery?
I have fallen into the snare of fate.
I laid my plan, but I was outwitted
from the start by the cunning of destiny.
How fortunate are the humbly born.   580
They can shed tears when they need to, they can tell
all their grief. But those of our station
are not allowed to appear
undignified. We are the slaves of the mob we lead,
molded by the pomp we must show in public.
I am ashamed
of my tears. But in the presence of this
enormity I am ashamed not to weep.
And my wife—
what words can I find, when I see her? How   590
will I greet her? With what eyes
will I welcome her? It was terrible
enough. Why did she have to come here too
when I never sent for her? But it is natural
for her to come here with her daughter,
to be present, the bride's mother,

to give her child in marriage.
And that's how she will learn of my treachery.
But the unhappy
girl. Girl? Why do I call her a girl?   600
When it seems that Hades
is about to make her his wife. Oh I
pity her. I can hear her
calling out to me, "Father!
Are you going to kill me? I hope that you
and everyone you love are married like this."
And Orestes will be there too, scarcely
old enough to walk, and he will
scream cries without words,
but my heart will know what they mean.   610
Oh what ruin Priam's son
Paris has brought me! All this he called down
by winning the love of Helen.

CHORUS   Grief lays hands on me too,
          though I am a stranger, and a woman, and these
          are a king's troubles.

MENELAOS Brother, give me your hand.

AGAMEMNON Here is my hand. You have won. I must bear
          the loss.

MENELAOS I swear by Pelops, whom our father   620
          called "Father," and by Atreus himself
          who sired us both, that I will
          speak to you now openly, as I feel,
          without any hidden object in mind,
          but speaking from my heart. When I saw the tears
          running from your eyes
          I felt tears of my own
          and pity. I will not set myself against you
          any longer. I call back what I said before.
          I am with you now, and I add my voice   630

43

to yours: do not
kill your child, not for my sake.
It cannot be just for you to suffer
so that I can be satisfied,
nor for your children to die
while mine fill their eyes with the light.
What do I need after all? Could I not find
a wife who would do me credit
if I chose to marry again? Am I to lose
a brother, whom I should treasure, merely to win back   640
Helen,
buying evil with good?
I was rash. I behaved like a child, until
I came close to the thing itself
and saw what it means, to kill one's own child.
Then pity overcame me. For the girl
from my own family who was going to lose her life
because of my marriage. What has your daughter
to do with Helen? Let the army
break up and leave Aulis. Brother,   650
no more tears, now. Yours are the cause of mine.
Whatever the oracles say of your daughter,
from now on it concerns you, not me.
I give you my share in it. You can see how long
my threats lasted. I admit
I changed my mind. But that's
natural if a man loves his brother.
At every step I've tried to see
the right way to act.
That's not the vacillation of a weakling.   660

CHORUS   Your words are noble. They are worthy
         of your ancestors.
         Tantalos himself, the son of Zeus,
         might well have been proud of them.

AGAMEMNON   Menelaos, thank you. I never could have hoped
            that you would speak as you have spoken now.

44

But what you have said is right
and worthy of you. Discord
flares up between brothers
over love or the family estate.   670
It is poisonous to both sides. I hate it.
But I have reached a point where circumstances
leave me no choice. I shall be
forced to shed her blood,
to kill my daughter.

MENELAOS Forced? Who can make you kill the girl?

AGAMEMNON The combined armies of the Achaians.

MENELAOS Not if you've sent her home
to Argos.

AGAMEMNON I might be able to do that   680
without anyone knowing. But afterwards—

MENELAOS What? You're wrong
to go in such dread of the mob.

AGAMEMNON Kalchas will tell the whole army
what was prophesied.

MENELAOS Not if he's dead. And that's a simple matter.

AGAMEMNON The tribe of prophets wants only to be important,
the whole rotten crowd of them.

MENELAOS When they don't prophesy
they're useless, and when they do   690
it does no good.

AGAMEMNON But aren't you afraid of something,
something I've just remembered?

MENELAOS Not unless you tell me what it is.

AGAMEMNON Someone else
knows everything. The son of Sisyphos,
Odysseus.

MENELAOS There's no reason for Odysseus
to do anything to injure you or me.

AGAMEMNON He's cunning, and it always turns out   700
that he and the crowd are on the same side.

MENELAOS He loves power. A terrible love.

AGAMEMNON Can't you see him rising
to his feet in the middle of the Argives
and repeating
the oracles that Kalchas spelled out to us,
telling how I promised
the sacrifice to Artemis
and then failed to keep my promise?
Can't you see   710
his words sweeping the whole army along with him
when he tells them
to kill you, kill me, and then sacrifice the girl them-
                                                        selves?
Even if I
could escape to Argos, they would follow me there.
They'd tear the city to the ground,
even the great walls that the Cyclopes built.
You see why I'm in despair. Almighty gods, how helpless
you have made me now!
There is nothing I can do. But you, Menelaos,   720
when you go back to the camp,
save me from one thing at least.
Take care that Clytemnestra
learns nothing of all this,
until I take my child and give her to Hades.

46

Let me suffer my ordeal
with as few tears as possible.
And you, women of Chalkis,
you will do well to say nothing.

MENELAOS *goes off left.* AGAMEMNON *goes in at the*
                                          central door.

CHORUS Blessed are they   730
        who share the delights of Aphrodite
        and are not burned alive by them, moderate
        and happy,
        whom the passion has not stung into madness, at
                                              whom
        the archer with the golden hair,
        Eros, has not aimed
        desire in his two arrows, the one
        striking rapture, the other
        devastation. Oh Cyprian,
        most beautiful of the goddesses, keep   7
        such wild flights from me.
        Let me know love
        within reason, and desire within
        marriage, and feel your presence
        not your rage.
        The natures of humans
        are various, and human ways of acting
        are different,
        but everyone knows what is right,
        and teaching   750
        inclines them at last to virtue.
        Humility is wisdom,
        making us see the right way
        as something beautiful.
        And from this beauty honor is born
        and life earns immortal fame.
        It is a great thing, the pursuit of virtue:
        in women it is a stillness

in their love;
among men, multiplied   760
ten thousand times among citizens,
it makes a city great.
Oh Paris, they took you as a baby
to grow up herding white heifers on Mount Ida,
making on reeds a barbarous
music, a thin echo
of the Phrygian pipes of Olympos.
The milk-laden cattle
never stopped grazing when the goddesses
stood forth for you to judge their beauty.   770
You chose
madness, and madness brought you
here to Greece, to the palace
inlaid with ivory,
and to the eyes of Helen
that took your gaze full of love and returned it.
And from that rose the dispute that sends
the armed Greeks in their ships
to sack Troy.

CLYTEMNESTRA, IPHIGENEIA, and ORESTES enter in a
          chariot escorted by the CHORUS OF ATTENDANTS.

CHORUS OF Oh great is the fortune   780
ATTENDANTS of the great!
          See, the king's daughter, Iphigeneia,
          my queen.
          And Tyndareos' daughter, Clytemnestra. How great
          were their ancestors! How momentous
          the occasion that brings them here!
          Those who excel in power and in wealth
          are gods, in the eyes
          of mortals less favored by fortune.

CHORUS OF (moving to the chariot) Let us stand here, women of
   WOMEN   Chalkis,   790

48

and hand the queen down from her chariot.
Make sure she does not stumble.
Gently, carefully, help with our hands,
let us help Agamemnon's
noble child to
descend unafraid for her first steps in Aulis.
(*to the occupants of the chariot*) We too are strangers
here. Gently, quietly,
we welcome the strangers from Argos.

CLYTEMNESTRA I think your kind greeting is a good omen.
I have come here bringing   800
this girl, as I hope, to a happy marriage.

To the ATTENDANTS.

Take from the chariot
the gifts I brought with her, her dowry.
Carry them in and set them down carefully.

The ATTENDANTS *carry the gifts into the tent.*

Daughter, come from the chariot, alight
on your delicate feet. And you,
young women, give her your arms, help her down.
Someone do the same for me,
as I step from the chariot. Someone stand
in front of the horses' yoke.   810
A colt's eye takes fright
if there is no one to reassure it.
This is Agamemnon's son. The baby
Orestes. Take him.
Are you still asleep, my child,
lulled by the rocking of the chariot?
When you wake, wake happily. This is your sister's
wedding day. You had
noble forebears, you will have

49

a noble kinsman: the sea-nymph's son   620
who is like his ancestors the gods.

CLYTEMNESTRA *hands* ORESTES *to a member of the
Chorus, descends, takes Orestes again, and sets him
down at her feet. As she speaks the next lines* AGA-
MEMNON *enters through the main door.*

Sit here by my feet, child. Iphigeneia,
come to your mother. Stand close
and show these strangers
what reason I have to be happy. Now
here comes your dear father. Greet him.

IPHIGENEIA *(starts to run to* AGAMEMNON, *then turns to* CLYTEM-
NESTRA*)* Mother, don't be angry
if I run from you
to be the first to embrace him.

CLYTEMNESTRA *(speaking at the same time)*
Oh most revered in my eyes, Agamemnon, King,   830
you commanded us to come, and we are here.

IPHIGENEIA *(running to* AGAMEMNON*)*
I want to run and put my arms around you,
Father, after such a long time!
How I have missed your face! Don't be angry!

CLYTEMNESTRA It's as it should be, child. You were always,
of all the children I bore him, the one
who loved your father most.

IPHIGENEIA Father, how happy I am to see you.
It has been so long.

AGAMEMNON And I am happy to see you, Iphigeneia.   840
The same words rise to my lips.

50

IPHIGENEIA Oh, if you could be as happy as I am! Father,
what a wonderful thing
to have brought me here to you.

AGAMEMNON Perhaps my child. Perhaps.

IPHIGENEIA How troubled your eyes look, yet you say
you are happy to see me.

AGAMEMNON A king and a general
has many burdens.

IPHIGENEIA Oh forget them, forget them for now. I am here.   850
Put them aside and be with me.

AGAMEMNON I am with you. I am nowhere else.

IPHIGENEIA Then don't frown any more.
I want those lines to leave your face.

AGAMEMNON See. How happy I am to look at you.

IPHIGENEIA But your eyes are overflowing with tears.

AGAMEMNON We will be separated
for so long.

IPHIGENEIA I don't understand what you mean.
Dear father, I don't understand.   860

AGAMEMNON If you understood I would feel even worse.

IPHIGENEIA Then we'll talk and I won't understand,
if that will make you happier.

AGAMEMNON Oh! (aside) I can't contain my suffering!
(aloud) Thank you.

51

IPHIGENEIA Stay home, Father. Stay with your children.

AGAMEMNON I want to. But I can't do what I
                      want to
                      and it makes me unhappy.

IPHIGENEIA Oh I wish there were no more   870
                      spears, no more
                      of this grievance that's come to Menelaos!

AGAMEMNON Before they are done
                      they will destroy others as they have me.

IPHIGENEIA Father, how long you've been
                      shut away in Aulis!

AGAMEMNON And even now something
                      prevents me from sending the army on its way.

IPHIGENEIA Where do they say
                      the Trojans live, Father?   880

AGAMEMNON In the country where Priam has a son,
                      a son named Paris
                      who I wish had never been born.

IPHIGENEIA You are going all that way, Father,
                      leaving me behind.

AGAMEMNON Now you see
                      what you did not understand before.

IPHIGENEIA Oh if only it were proper for me to go with you!

AGAMEMNON You will think of your father
                      on your own long voyage.   890

IPHIGENEIA Will my mother come with me
                      or will I be alone?

AGAMEMNON Neither father nor mother. Alone.

IPHIGENEIA You won't make me live
somewhere else, will you, Father?

AGAMEMNON I have said enough. Too much. Girls
are not meant to know about such things.

IPHIGENEIA When you have finished what you have to do
at Troy, Father,
sail straight home to me.   900

AGAMEMNON Before that
I must make a sacrifice. Here in Aulis.

IPHIGENEIA Sacrifices are to find out
how we may please the gods.

AGAMEMNON You will see. You will stand by the font
of purifying water.

IPHIGENEIA Will we dance around the altar?

AGAMEMNON How I envy you, knowing nothing!
Now go in. It's better
for young girls not to be seen.   910
Give me a kiss, and your right hand.
You will soon be far away from your father,
and for a long time.
Oh breast, cheeks, oh blonde head,
what a crushing weight
Helen and the Trojan city
have called down upon you!
I must not touch you any more.
It sets the tears flowing. Go in.

IPHIGENEIA *goes in at the left-hand door.*

Daughter of Leda, forgive me   920

53

for this access of grief
at giving my child in marriage to Achilles.
Partings such as these are happy, of course,
but when a father must send
his daughter to the house of another
after all his years of watching over her
it cuts into the heart.

CLYTEMNESTRA I feel it too. I'm not so foolish as to reproach you
for grieving. I will feel just the same,
you know, when I lead the child   930
out into the marriage hymns,
so I don't blame you.
But time will heal the sadness. It's the custom and
we will get used to it. Tell me
about his ancestors, and where he was born.
All I know is his name.

AGAMEMNON To Asopos
a daughter was born, named Aigina.

CLYTEMNESTRA Who married her? A mortal, a god?

AGAMEMNON Zeus himself. And she bore him a son,   940
Aiakos, king of the island of Oinone.

CLYTEMNESTRA And which of his children succeeded him?

AGAMEMNON Peleus. He married one of the daughters
of Nereus, the sea-god.

CLYTEMNESTRA With her father's blessings, or did Peleus
take her in defiance of the gods?

AGAMEMNON Zeus made the betrothal, and gave her in marriage.
He has the authority.

CLYTEMNESTRA Where were they married?
Under the waves of the ocean?   950

AGAMEMNON At the foot of Pelion,
the sacred mountain where Cheiron lives.

CLYTEMNESTRA In the country where they say the centaurs live?

AGAMEMNON There all the gods came to the marriage of Peleus
and the wedding feast.

CLYTEMNESTRA And was it Thetis or his father Peleus
who brought Achilles up?

AGAMEMNON It was Cheiron,
to keep him from learning the evil ways of men.

CLYTEMNESTRA Wise teacher! And Peleus was wiser still,   960
sending the boy to him.

AGAMEMNON Such is the man who will be your daughter's husband.

CLYTEMNESTRA He sounds acceptable. Where in Greece is he from?

AGAMEMNON From Phthia, on the river Apidanos.

CLYTEMNESTRA And that is where he will take our daughter?

AGAMEMNON That is for him to decide.

CLYTEMNESTRA May it be a happy marriage!
When will it take place?

AGAMEMNON At the full moon.
That is the most propitious time.   970

CLYTEMNESTRA Have you made our daughter's
sacrifice to the goddess?

AGAMEMNON I will. We had just come to that.

CLYTEMNESTRA And afterwards you will have the marriage feast?

55

AGAMEMNON When I have offered the gods
the sacrifice they require of me.

CLYTEMNESTRA And where shall I prepare the women's banquet?

AGAMEMNON Here. By the high sterns of the ships from Argos.

CLYTEMNESTRA Here? Well, there is no choice. I hope
good fortune comes of it.   980

AGAMEMNON Do you know what you should do?
Please do it.

CLYTEMNESTRA What do you want? You know I'm not in the habit
of disobeying you.

AGAMEMNON Then here, in the presence of the bridegroom,
we men will—

CLYTEMNESTRA You? Will I not be there
for the things a bride's mother must do?

AGAMEMNON I will give away your child. The army and I.

CLYTEMNESTRA And where will I be when that happens?   990

AGAMEMNON In Argos, taking care of your daughters.

CLYTEMNESTRA Leaving my child here? And who
will raise the bridal torch?

AGAMEMNON I will provide the light, all the light
proper for the bridal pair.

CLYTEMNESTRA That is wrong, wrong. And such things are important.

AGAMEMNON It is not right for you to stay here
jostling among the soldiers.

CLYTEMNESTRA It is right that I should give
my children in marriage. I am their mother.   1000

AGAMEMNON It is not right for our daughters at home
to be left alone.

CLYTEMNESTRA They are well looked after,
safe in their part of the palace.

AGAMEMNON Please do it.

CLYTEMNESTRA No, by the goddess who reigns in Argos.
You see to the things outside
that concern you. I'll go in
and see to the preparations for my daughter's wedding.

She goes in at the left-hand door.

AGAMEMNON Oh, it was no use. I tried but I failed   1010
to send my wife out of my sight.
I contrive plots, I lay plans to deceive
those dearest to me
and it all comes to nothing.
Now I must arrange with Kalchas, who performs
our sacrifices,
the thing which the goddess demands
and I hate the thought of.
I owe it to Greece.
A wise man supports in his house   1020
a good and faithful wife. Or no wife at all.

He goes off left.

CHORUS Now they will sail
to Simoïs where the waters spin silver,
the Greeks in pride of numbers,
of ships, of weapons. They will come
to Ilion, to the plains below Troy
shining in the blessing of Apollo,

where Kassandra, they say, flings
like sunlight the blonde falls of her hair
from under the green laurel when the god   1030
grips her and she shakes
and sees what is to come.
At Troy on the ramparts, on the circling
walls, drawn up,
the Trojans will be waiting
as Ares in his bronze battle gear
comes nearer with the falling oars,
the hanging prows riffling the estuary mouths
of Simoïs. What he will want
is Helen, the sister   1040
of the twin sons of Zeus, the Dioskouroi,
who are stars in heaven.
To possess her again out of Priam's kingdom,
the prize
of the Achaians' spears, shields, labors in battle,
and bring her once more into Greece.
The god will girdle with slaughter
the stone-cased stronghold
of Pergamos, the Phrygians' city. He will see
Priam's head hewn from its shoulders   1050
and every house in Troy
smashed and rummaged. Then what a crying
from the girls and from Priam's queen.
And Helen herself, the daughter of Zeus,
will taste tears for the day she left her husband.
Oh may such anguish never befall us,
women of Chalkis, nor our children's children,
as shall then work through the Lydian women
for all their gold,
and through the wives of Phrygia so that they   1060
stand by the looms saying, "Who now
will wrap his wrist in my swaying hair and uproot me
out of my ruined home,
dragging me through my tears?
It is all thanks to you, daughter

of the swan with the sinuous neck, whose wings
hid Zeus from Leda,
if that is true.
It is still you
even if that is no more than a story   1070
out of the books of the Muses,
with no meaning."

Enter ACHILLES *left, unarmed and dressed with osten-*
tatious simplicity. He looks about twenty-five years old.

ACHILLES Where is the commander of the Achaians?
Will one of his servants tell him that Peleus' son
Achilles is standing at his door?
It is not the same for all of us
having to wait here
by the straits. Some of us,
who have no wives, sit here by the shore, having left
empty houses at home. Others, who are married,   1080
still have no children.
Such is the frenzy that has seized Greece
for this war,
not without the consent of the gods.
With things at this pass, let me say,
what is due to me. Anyone else who wants to
may speak in his own behalf. I came away
from Pharsalia, I left Peleus,
to be kept waiting for
a wind, beside the straits,   1090
trying to keep my men quiet, my Myrmidons:
day after day they come up to me and say, "Achilles,
what is keeping us here? How much more
time must we waste on this expedition to Troy?
Do what you came here to do
or else lead the army home.
Don't wait for the sons of Atreus."

CLYTEMNESTRA *enters from the left-hand door.*

59

CLYTEMNESTRA Son of the Nereïd, I heard your voice
and came out to greet you.

ACHILLES Oh sacred modesty, who   1100
is this beautiful woman?

CLYTEMNESTRA You could hardly expect to recognize me
since you never saw me before,
but your regard for modesty is commendable.

ACHILLES Who are you? And why have you come
to the camp of the Greek army,
you a woman, here among the shields?

CLYTEMNESTRA I am the daughter of Leda,
Clytemnestra. Agamemnon is my husband.

ACHILLES Brief and to the point.   1110
But it is not seemly for me
to be seen talking with women.

He starts to go off left.

CLYTEMNESTRA Wait. Why do you run away? (*following him*)
Give me your right hand—here is mine:
a happy beginning to this betrothal of ours!

ACHILLES (*turns politely, then recoils in horror*) Do you know
what you are saying? Touch
your hand? How could I face Agamemnon
if I touch what heaven forbids me to touch?

CLYTEMNESTRA Why do you say heaven forbids it,
son of Thetis the sea-nymph,   1120
when you are about to marry my daughter?

ACHILLES Marry? Lady, what do you mean?
I am left with no answer. Has some delusion
led your mind astray?

CLYTEMNESTRA I know it is natural
              for men to be shy, faced with new kin
              and the talk of marriage.

ACHILLES Lady, I have never courted your daughter,
          and the sons of Atreus have not spoken
          one word to me about marriage.   1130

CLYTEMNESTRA What does this mean?
              Indeed my words must be as shocking to you
              as your words are shocking to me.

ACHILLES We must both find the explanation. There must be
          some truth under what we both said.

CLYTEMNESTRA I have been deceived. It seems
              I have been preparing a marriage
              that exists only in my mind.
              I am filled with shame.

ACHILLES Perhaps someone is amusing himself   1140
          with both of us.
          Ignore it. It doesn't matter.

CLYTEMNESTRA I will take my leave. I am humiliated.
              I have been made to lie.
              I can no longer look you in the face.

                    She starts to go in at the left-hand door.

ACHILLES Lady, good-bye. I shall go in
          to see your husband.

          *He starts to go in at the main entrance, then pauses as
          he hears the OLD MAN call through the right-hand
          door. CLYTEMNESTRA pauses also.*

OLD MAN (off) Wait, stranger! Grandson of Aiakos,
         son of the goddess, you
         I'm calling, and you, daughter of Leda.   1150

61

ACHILLES Who is that, shouting through the doorway?
          How shaken he sounds!

OLD MAN I am a slave. That's the truth, why not say it?
         Fate has given me no choice.

ACHILLES Whose slave? Not mine, certainly, here
          among Agamemnon's possessions.

OLD MAN That lady's, in front of the tent.
         I was given to her by Tyndareos, her father.

ACHILLES Well, here I am. Why did you want me to stay?

OLD MAN Is there no one else here   1160
         besides you and her?

ACHILLES We are alone. Come out from the king's tent. Speak.

OLD MAN What I most feared has come to pass. Oh destiny,
         (entering) spare those I pray for!

ACHILLES Your words sound ominous,
          and the message, it seems, is important.

CLYTEMNESTRA Don't wait to kiss my hand. What did you want to
                                                              tell me?

OLD MAN You know me, lady. You know my
         devotion to you and your children.

CLYTEMNESTRA I know you've been a servant in the palace   1170
              for a long time.

OLD MAN I came to King Agamemnon
         as part of your dowry.

CLYTEMNESTRA Yes, you came with us to Argos
              and you've always belonged to me.

62

OLD MAN I have. And I put your interests
ahead of your husband's.

CLYTEMNESTRA Now tell us. What is your secret?

OLD MAN Your daughter. Her father
is going to kill her.   1180
With his own hand.

CLYTEMNESTRA What? I spit against what you say, old man!
You're out of your senses!

OLD MAN He will plunge a blade into her white throat.

CLYTEMNESTRA Oh, torment! Has he gone mad?

OLD MAN No, he is sane about everything except you
and your child. There he's lost his reason.

CLYTEMNESTRA Why? What demon could prompt him to such a
thing?

OLD MAN The oracle. According to Kalchas. Saying
what must happen before the fleet can sail.   1190

CLYTEMNESTRA What horror is coming to me, and the child
whose father will kill her! Sail where?

OLD MAN To the country of Dardanos, for Menelaos
to bring back Helen.

CLYTEMNESTRA So the fates have woven Iphigeneia's death
into Helen's homecoming?

OLD MAN Now you know it all. He intends
to sacrifice your daughter to Artemis.

CLYTEMNESTRA And the talk of marriage, which brought me here?

63

OLD MAN The king knew you would bring her, and gladly,   1200
to marry Achilles.

CLYTEMNESTRA Oh daughter, you have come here
to your death, and your mother with you.

OLD MAN The child's fate is terrible. So is yours.
It is a monstrous decision, Agamemnon's.

CLYTEMNESTRA I am helpless. I am lost. Whatever I do
the tears come.

OLD MAN If losing a child is painful, you have
reason for tears.

CLYTEMNESTRA But where did you learn all this, old man?   1210
How did it come to your ears?

OLD MAN I was sent to you with a second letter
about the first one.

CLYTEMNESTRA Telling me again to bring the girl here
to die, or warning me not to?

OLD MAN Warning you not to. At that moment
your husband was in his right mind.

CLYTEMNESTRA If you had such a letter for me
why was it not delivered?

OLD MAN Menelaos took it from me.   1220
All your troubles come from him.

CLYTEMNESTRA Son of Thetis and Peleus,
have you heard this?

ACHILLES I have heard the cause of your grief,
and I do not take lightly
the way I have been involved in the matter.

CLYTEMNESTRA They are going to kill my child.
They tricked her with this talk of marrying you.

ACHILLES I too blame Agamemnon,
and not only for the reasons you speak of.   1230

CLYTEMNESTRA (*dropping to her knees and embracing* ACHILLES' *legs*)
Son of a goddess, I, a mortal,
am not ashamed to clasp your knees. What good
would pride do me now? What matters more to me
than my daughter's life?
Son of a goddess, save us: me
in my wretchedness,
and Iphigeneia, who they said was your betrothed,
even though it was not true.
I myself put the bridal wreath on her head for you,
I brought her here to be married,   1240
and now I am leading her to her death.
You will be blamed if you do nothing to defend her.

She rises, puts her left hand to ACHILLES' *cheek and
takes his right hand in her own.*

Even though you were never married to her
you were called her husband.
I implore you by your beard, by your right hand,
by your own mother. Your name, Achilles,
destroyed me; now you must clear it.

Kneels and takes his knees again.

There is no altar where I can take refuge,
none except your knees.
No friend smiles on me here. You have heard   1250
of Agamemnon's raw heartlessness.
Nothing is sacred to him.
And I am a woman, come
into a camp of sailors, hard to control

and ripe for any crime—though they can be
useful enough when they want to be.
If you can bring yourself to stretch out
your hand over me, we are saved.
If not, we are lost.

CHORUS   Giving birth is a mystery. It casts   1260
a powerful spell over mothers. All, all of them
without exception
will risk any suffering
for the sake of one of their children.

ACHILLES   Pride rises up in me
and draws me on. But I have learned
to curb my grief in adversity, and my joy
in triumph.
Mortals who have learned this
can hope to live by reason. There are moments   1270
when it is good not to be too wise,
but there are times too when taking thought is useful.
I was brought up in the house of Cheiron,
the most righteous of men,
and he taught me to act from a simple heart.
If the commands of the sons of Atreus
are just, I will obey them. If not,
I will refuse. But whether here
or in Troy, I will remain free,
and in my fighting will bring credit on the war god   1280
with my whole strength. As for you,
you have been treated cruelly
by those closest to you,
and as far as is proper for me, I shall extend
my pity to cover you. Never shall your daughter,
who has been called my betrothed,
be slaughtered by her father. He shall not use
me in his manipulations.
That way my name would be her butcher
as surely as if it had drawn the sword.   1290

66

Your husband is the cause of this, but my own
body would be defiled
if through me that girl were to die,
horribly, brutally used, as she
has been. It fills me with rage
to think how she has been treated. I would be
the lowest of the Argives, a nothing,
and Menelaos a hero,
I would be no son of Peleus, but some
demon's offspring, if I   1300
let my name do your husband's killing for him.
I swear by Nereus, whom the waves cradled, father
of Thetis who gave me birth,
King Agamemnon shall not touch your daughter
nor so much as graze her gown
with his finger-tips,
or that barbarous settlement in Lydia,
Sipylos, where his sires
first saw the light,
is a Grecian city,   1310
and no one has heard of Phthia.
This Kalchas, their prophet, will find
a bitter taste in the barley
and the lustral water before that sacrifice.
What is a prophet? Someone
who utters one truth in a flock of lies,
if he's lucky, and if he's not
everybody forgets.
I'm not saying this to earn a bride.
There are thousands I could marry.   1320
But I will not suffer this insult from King Agamemnon.
He should have asked my permission
if he wanted to use me to lure the girl here
into his snare,
since it was to see her married to me
that Clytemnestra would have brought her most will-
                                                            ingly.
I would have lent the use of my name

67

to the Greeks,
so that the ships could sail to Ilion.
I am here with the others. It is the same war.   1330
I would not have refused to help.
But I have been treated by these commanders
as though I were nobody. They accord me their
honor or they ignore me as they please.
My sword may decide that. Blood will color it
before we sail to Phrygia
if anyone thinks to take your daughter from me.
Be calm. In your time of danger, suddenly
I appeared to you as if I were some great god.
I am not. But to save the girl,   1340
I will be.

CHORUS Son of Peleus, what you have said is worthy
        of you, worthy of the proud sea-goddess
        and her son.

CLYTEMNESTRA How can I find the right praise,
              neither cloying with flattery, nor so meager
              that it offends you? Men of worth
              have a way of hating those who praise them too much.
              I am ashamed to enlarge on my sufferings.
              They are mine, they do not concern you. Still,   1350
              even if their afflictions are not his, a good man
              may help those in trouble. Take pity on us.
              Our plight deserves it. First I thought
              you would be my son—an empty hope, as I learned.
              Now my child is threatened with death:
              a bad augury for your marriage one day,
              unless you take steps to protect yourself.
              But why do I urge you? From beginning to end
              you have spoken nobly. My child
              will be saved, if you can save her. Would it please you   1360
              if she came and embraced your knees as a suppliant?
              True, it is not seemly for a girl to do so,
              but if you wished she would come

with dignity, and eyes cast down. And yet
if my supplication alone
can move you
I would rather she were not called.
She is over-timid, perhaps. But all forms
of modesty
are worth respecting.   1370

ACHILLES Do not bring your daughter
here for me to see. Why should we incur
the comments of the ignorant?
An army crowded together, loosed from work at home,
will gossip and spread foul stories.
Whether you supplicate me or not, you come
to the same end. For me
the one thing of importance
is to save you from disaster.
And this you may count on: I never lie.   1380
May I die if I deceive you. And live
only if she does.

CLYTEMNESTRA May you be blessed all your days
for helping those who are unhappy.

ACHILLES We must lay plans. Listen.

CLYTEMNESTRA Go on. I need no urging to listen to you.

ACHILLES Let us try to make her father see reason.

CLYTEMNESTRA He is too cowardly. He is afraid of the army.

ACHILLES Arguments can beat down arguments.

CLYTEMNESTRA A cold hope. But what do you want mè to do?   1390

ACHILLES First, plead with him not to kill his daughter.
If he refuses you, then you can come to me,

but you may persuade him
by yourself.
Then there would be no need for my help.
You are safe, in any case. And there would be
no breach, then, in my friendship with Agamemnon,
no cause for the army to reproach me,
no weapon used to bring it about,
only reason. So it would turn out well for you   1400
and those dear to you
and I would not be forced to act.

CLYTEMNESTRA How wise you are! I will do as you say. But suppose
something goes wrong: where
and how will I see you again?
Shall I come, in my misery, searching
for your hand to rescue us?

ACHILLES I will be watching, in the right place.
You will not have to be stared at
hunting through the troops to find me. Do nothing   1410
that would disgrace your fathers.
Tyndareos should not suffer shame.
He was a great man in Greece.

CLYTEMNESTRA You are right. Lead me. I ask only
to be your slave.
If there are gods the gods will reward your goodness.
If there are none what does anything matter?

CLYTEMNESTRA goes in at the left door, the OLD MAN
at the right. ACHILLES goes off left.

CHORUS Oh what a sound of Libyan flutes,
of lyres leading the dance, of reeling
reeds raised the marriage hymn   1420
on Pelion, when the Muses
came robed in their bright hair to the banquet
with the gods, and their gold

sandals stamped the ground
on the way to the marriage of Peleus,
and their voices
carried over the centaurs' slopes, and through
the woods of Pelion, praise
of Thetis and Aiakos' son.
There Dardanos' child,   1430
Trojan Ganymede, the darling of Zeus, poured out
mixed wine from the deep bowls of gold,
and in celebration the fifty
daughters of Nereus turned
their braided dance on the white sand
of the shore.
And the centaurs came
riding, with pine spears and crowned with leaves,
to the feast of the gods, and the bowl
that Bakchos filled, and they cried, "Daughter   1440
of Nereus, great
is the son you will bear:
a light and a splendor to Thessaly,
as Cheiron, who knows
the oracles of Apollo, foretells,
saying that your child will sail with an army
of Myrmidons, and their spears, to the land of Troy
to burn King Priam's glorious city,
his limbs traced
in gold armor wrought for him   1450
by the god Hephaistos,
the gift of his mother Thetis, the sea-goddess."
So the gods celebrated the marriage of Peleus
and the first-born of the Nereïds.
But you, Iphigeneia, on your
lovely hair the Argives will set
a wreath, as on the brows
of a spotted heifer, led down
from caves in the mountains
to the sacrifice,   1460
and the knife will open the throat

and let the blood of a girl.
And you were not
brought up to the sound of the shepherd's pipe
and the cries of the herdsmen,
but nurtured by your mother
to be a bride for one of great Inachos' sons.
Oh where is the noble face
of modesty, or the strength of virtue, now
that blasphemy is in power   1470
and men have put justice
behind them, and there is no law but lawlessness,
and none join in fear of the gods?

                    CLYTEMNESTRA *enters from the left-hand door.*

CLYTEMNESTRA I have come out looking for my husband.
             He has been away from here for some time. My
                                                      daughter,
             poor child, has learned
             of the death her father plans for her.
             One minute she is shaken with sobbing
             and the next the tears
             flow almost in silence.   1480
             But it was Agamemnon I named: here he is.
             He will soon stand convicted
             of planning a crime against his own child.

                    AGAMEMNON *enters left, alone.*

AGAMEMNON Daughter of Leda, I am glad
          that we meet out here,
          for I must speak to you now of things that a bride
          should not hear.

CLYTEMNESTRA It's a good moment for that.

AGAMEMNON Call the child out to her father.
          The libations are ready, and the barley grains   1490

72

ready to be thrown into the purifying flame,
and the calves that must loose
to Artemis their dark blood
to bless the marriage.

CLYTEMNESTRA You find innocent words to describe it
but there are no words
for what you have decided. (*She calls in at the left
door.*) Come, child.
You know what your father means to do.
Wrap the baby Orestes
in your robe and bring him with you.   1500

IPHIGENEIA *enters from the left door, carrying* ORESTES.
With her free hand she covers her face with her robe.
CLYTEMNESTRA *too keeps her face turned from* AGA-
MEMNON.

Here she is, obedient to your command.
For the rest,
I will answer for us both.

AGAMEMNON Why are you crying, child? Aren't you still happy
to see me? Why are you holding your robe
in front of your eyes,
with your face turned to the ground?

CLYTEMNESTRA I cannot think where
to start my bitter story,
for its beginning is grief,   1510
its middle is grief,
its end
is grief.

AGAMEMNON What is it? Why are all three of you
afraid to look at me?

CLYTEMNESTRA My husband,

find the honesty of a man
and answer me with it.

AGAMEMNON   There is no need for you to speak that way.
Ask me your question.   1520

CLYTEMNESTRA   Do you intend to kill your daughter?

AGAMEMNON   What a horrible thing to ask! What a vile suspicion!

CLYTEMNESTRA   Simply answer the question.

AGAMEMNON   Any reasonable question I would answer.

CLYTEMNESTRA   This question. This is the only one I care about.

AGAMEMNON   Oh immovable law of heaven! Oh my
anguish, my relentless fate!

CLYTEMNESTRA   Yours? Mine. Hers. No relenting for any of us.

AGAMEMNON   How have you been wronged?

CLYTEMNESTRA   How can you ask? What a question   1530
for a man of sense!

AGAMEMNON   (to himself) I am lost. Someone has betrayed me.

CLYTEMNESTRA   I know the whole story. I have found out
what you mean to do to me.
Your silence itself is a confession.
So is your sighing. No need to waste words.

AGAMEMNON   Then I will say nothing. What good would it do
to lie, and add shamelessness to my troubles?

CLYTEMNESTRA   Listen to me, then. I will use plain words, and not
talk in riddles. In the first place   1540

you took me by force, you married me
against my will.
You killed the husband I had, Tantalos.
You ripped from my breast
my baby, still
living, you smashed it on the ground.
Then when my brothers, the sons
of Zeus, on their shining horses,
bore down on you bringing war,
you came on your knees to my old father   1550
Tyndareos, and he saved you.
So you got me for your wife, again.
I came to love you. Admit
that as your wife I have deserved no reproach.
My demands in love have been modest. I have done
what I could to increase your house
so that you would be glad to come home, and you
                                                    went out
proud and at peace. It is not often
that a man acquires a good wife.
There is no end of the other kind. And I bore you   1560
this son, and three daughters, and now
you have the cruelty
to take one of these from me.
And if anyone asks you
why you intend to kill her, what will you say?
Shall I answer for you? So that Menelaos
can have Helen back. Strange
bargain: you'll pay your child's life
as the price of a worthless woman.
We'll buy back our own harm   1570
with what is most dear to us.
Now I want you to think of this. You'll sail
to the war, and I'll be left in the house.
You may be gone for years. There I'll be.
And with what heart, do you imagine, I will pass
my days in those halls, finding
all her places empty,

75

her girl's room empty of her forever, and
finding myself alone
with nothing but my tears and the endless   1580
grieving at her fate: "My child,
it was your own father who killed you.
No one else. That was his hand,
no one else's. That was his reward for love.
And after that, he will come home again."
Then almost any occasion
would serve, for my other children and me
to give you the welcome you will have earned.
In the name of the gods, don't force me to turn
against you. Don't wrong me yourself.   1590
As you kill our child what prayers will you be saying?
What blessing can you ask
as you have cut her throat? A bad voyage home,
since your setting out was the consequence of a crime?
And in justice, could I give you my blessing?
We would have to think the gods had no minds,
to pray for murderers.
And when you come back to Argos
will you kiss your children? It will be forbidden
by the gods. And which of the children   1600
will dare even to look at you? They will be afraid
that you will kiss them only to kill them.
Did any of that ever cross your mind? Or do you
think of nothing but waving scepters
and leading armies? Would it not have been fair
to say to the Achaians, "Men of Argos,
you want to sail to Troy. Draw lots. Let us see
whose daughter will die." That way would have had
its justice. There is none
in your offering up your daughter   1610
as a victim for the army. Or let Menelaos,
to whom it matters most, after all, cut his own
daughter's throat: Hermione's, for the sake
of her mother. But it is my own child
who is to be torn from me, when I have been

faithful to you,
while she who dishonored her husband's bed will find
her daughter safe at home, in Sparta,
and be happy. Now answer me,
tell me if one thing I've said is not true.   1620
But if there is justice and truth
in what I say, do not kill your daughter and mine.
Turn back, be wise.

CHORUS Do as she asks, Agamemnon.
It is good when people help each other,
to save children. Who can deny that?

IPHIGENEIA *hands* ORESTES *to her mother, then kneels*
and clasps AGAMEMNON's *knees.*

IPHIGENEIA If I had the tongue of Orpheus, Father, whose song
could charm stones so that they followed after him,
if my words could persuade
whoever I wished to whatever I wished, I would use   1630
all my arts now. But all that I know how to do
at this moment is cry. I offer you my tears.
I press against your knees
like a suppliant's torn branch, my body
which my mother bore you. Do not send me
into death before my time. It is sweet to see
the light. Do not make me look
at what is under the earth.
I was the first who called you father, the first
you called your child,   1640
the first to climb on your knees, and we
held each other, we loved each other. You said,
"Will I see you living in your husband's house,
enjoying the happiness that is my daughter's right?"
And I answered, touching your beard, as I do now—
but now as the gesture
of a suppliant—, "And what will I do for you
then, Father? When you are old

will you come to live with me,
and let me nurse your age, in return   1650
for what you have done for me?"
I remember what we said, but you have forgotten.
And now you want to kill me. Oh, in the name
of Pelops, of your father
Atreus, of my mother, suffering here
again as at my birth, do not let it happen.
What have I to do with Paris
and Helen, and what they have done?
Why should Paris' coming to Argos mean that I
must die? Look at me. In my eyes. Kiss me,   1660
so that at least I may remember that
when I am dying,
if you will not listen to what I say.

AGAMEMNON and IPHIGENEIA *kiss. As she speaks the fol-*
lowing lines IPHIGENEIA *takes* ORESTES *from* CLYTEM-
NESTRA *and holds him up to* AGAMEMNON.

My brother, you are so small
to have to help your friends. But cry
with me, cry to your father, beg him
not to kill your sister. See,
even babies sense the dread of evil to come.
Even without being able to speak, he cries to you,
begging. Take pity on me.   1670
Respect your daughter's life. Both of us,
your own blood, touch your beard,
imploring you: a baby,
a grown girl. In three words I can say it all:
the sweetest thing
we ever see is this daylight. Under the ground
there is nothing.
Only the mad choose to be dead. The meanest life
is better than the most glorious death.

She hands ORESTES *to* CLYTEMNESTRA.

CHORUS Oh reckless Helen, now from you   1680
        and your marriage
        a deadly struggle begins
        between the sons of Atreus and their children.

AGAMEMNON I know when pity is due, and when it is not.
        I love my children. Only the mad do not.
        Wife, it is terrible to me
        to bring myself to do this,
        and terrible if I do not.
        For I am forced to do it. (to IPHIGENEIA) Look: how
                                     many ships,
        the war fleet, assembled here, the proud men of Greece   1690
        and their bronze battle-gear, and they
        cannot sail to the towers
        of Ilion, and seize
        the famous citadel, Troy,
        according to Kalchas the prophet, unless I
        sacrifice you.
        Some strange Aphrodite has crazed
        the whole Greek army with a passion to sail at once
        to the barbarians' own country
        and end this piracy of Greek marriage.   1700
        If I disobey the goddess, if I ignore
        the oracle, then the army will sail to Argos,
        they will kill you and me, and your sisters
        who are still at home. I have not become
        Menelaos' creature. I am not guided by him.
        It is Greece that compels me
        to sacrifice you, whatever I wish.
        We are in stronger hands than our own.
        Greece must be free
        if you and I can make her so. Being Greeks,   1710
        we must not be subject to barbarians,
        we must not let them carry off our wives.

                                  He goes off left.

CLYTEMNESTRA Oh strangers, oh my daughter, now I see
your death! Your father is running away from you,
after giving you up to Hades.

IPHIGENEIA Oh mother, how can I bear it?
The same lamenting song
falls to us both, our fate.
I must say good-bye to the light. I will not
see the sun any more. Oh unlucky   1720
valley of Phrygia, filled with snow,
oh high slopes of Ida where Priam
once left a baby, torn from its mother,
to die: Paris, his own child, known
in time as the son of Ida,
Paris of Ida,
among the Phrygians. If only the herdsman
had not brought him up with the flocks,
not reared him, Paris, Alexander,
to watch his flock by the clear   1730
springs where the nymphs rise,
and the rich pastures starred
with roses and hyacinths
for the goddesses to gather.
It was there that Pallas came,
and seductive Cypris, and Hera, and with them
Hermes, the gods' messenger:
Cypris proud of the desires she wakens,
Pallas proud of her spear,
Hera proud of the bed of Zeus,   1740
came for the fatal judgment, vying in beauty,
whose issue is my death,
oh my friends,
whatever glory it brings to the Argives.
For I am to be the first sacrifice
to Artemis for the passage to Ilion.
And he who begot me has betrayed me and left me,
and I curse in my despair,
I curse the day that ever I saw you, Helen,   1750

for I am to be murdered, I am to fail
to my ungodly father's
ungodly knife. Oh if only
Aulis had never opened
her folded bay to the bronze-beaked galleys,
the fir keels that will ferry them to Troy,
or the breath of Zeus had not blown fair up the current
of Euripos. Sweetly he blows
on this man's sails and on that man's, making those
men
happy. To others he brings   1760
bad luck, bitter compulsion.
Some can set out on voyages, and some
can make port. Others must wait. Truly
we are creatures
of labor and suffering, and nothing for long.
Labor and suffering,
and the plain sight
of our destiny is the cruelest thing of all.

CHORUS Oh daughter of Tyndareos, what anguish,
what bitter sorrows   1770
you have called down on Greece!

(to IPHIGENEIA)

I pity you. You do not deserve your fate.

IPHIGENEIA (looking offstage, left) Mother, mother! I see men
coming.

CLYTEMNESTRA (looking in the same direction) Achilles too, child,
the son of the goddess,
in whose name you were brought here.

IPHIGENEIA (running to the left door and calling to the servants
inside) Women, open the doors so that I can hide.

CLYTEMNESTRA Why, child?

IPHIGENEIA I would be ashamed to see him.

CLYTEMNESTRA Why?

IPHIGENEIA I am ashamed of my unlucky marriage. 1780

CLYTEMNESTRA There is no time now for delicacy. Stay here.
Do not be shy. We must do what we can.

> Enter ACHILLES left, followed by attendants bearing
> his shield, spears, sword, breastplate, greaves, and
> helmet.

ACHILLES Unhappy daughter of Leda.

CLYTEMNESTRA Unhappy is what I am.

> Noise of shouting offstage.

ACHILLES The Argives are shouting.
They want a terrible thing.

CLYTEMNESTRA What are they shouting?

ACHILLES About your daughter.

CLYTEMNESTRA Your words have an unhappy beginning.

ACHILLES They say she must be sacrificed. 1790

CLYTEMNESTRA And will no one speak against them?

ACHILLES They shouted about me, too.

CLYTEMNESTRA What did they say?

ACHILLES "Stone him to death!"

CLYTEMNESTRA For trying to save my daughter?

ACHILLES For that.

CLYTEMNESTRA Who would have dared
to raise a hand against you?

ACHILLES Every Greek there.

CLYTEMNESTRA But your own army of Myrmidons,   1800
surely they took your side?

ACHILLES They were the first to threaten me.

CLYTEMNESTRA Oh my child, we are lost.

ACHILLES They said I was foolish about this marriage.

CLYTEMNESTRA What did you answer?

ACHILLES That they were not to kill my bride.

CLYTEMNESTRA Good.

ACHILLES Whom her father had promised to me.

CLYTEMNESTRA And brought here from Argos.

> More shouting offstage, left.

ACHILLFS Their voices drowned me out.   1810

CLYTEMNESTRA The mob. An infernal thing!

ACHILLES But I will defend you.

CLYTEMNESTRA You alone? Against the whole army?

> ACHILLES points to the armor-bearers.

ACHILLES See. These men are carrying my armor.

CLYTEMNESTRA May heaven reward your courage.

ACHILLES Heaven will.

CLYTEMNESTRA And my daughter will not be sacrificed?

ACHILLES Not if I can stop it.

CLYTEMNESTRA Will they come here to take the girl?

ACHILLES Thousands of them,   1820
     led by Odysseus.

CLYTEMNESTRA The son of Sisyphos?

ACHILLES That one.

CLYTEMNESTRA Did he offer to do it, or did the army choose him?

ACHILLES They chose him, but the choice pleased him.

CLYTEMNESTRA A vile choice: to be the accomplice
     in a murder.

ACHILLES I will stop him.

CLYTEMNESTRA Is he going to drag her away against her will?

ACHILLES By her blonde hair.   1830

CLYTEMNESTRA And what should I do then?

ACHILLES Hold on to her.

CLYTEMNESTRA You mean that will stop them
     from killing her?

ACHILLES That is what it will come to.

IPHIGENEIA Mother, both of you, listen to me.
          I see now that you are wrong
          to be angry with your husband.
          It is hard to hold out against the inevitable.
          The stranger deserves to be thanked   1840
          for being willing to help us, but on no account
          must we let the army be stirred up against him.
          It would not help us, and he might come to harm.
          Now mother, listen to the conclusion
          that I have reached. I have made up my mind to die.
          I want to come to it
          with glory, I want to have thrown off
          all weak and base thoughts. Mother,
          look at it with my eyes,
          and see how right I am.   1850
          All the people, all the strength of Greece
          have turned to me. All those ships,
          whether they sail, whether Troy falls,
          depend on me. I will be the one
          to protect our women, in the future,
          if ever the barbarians dare to come near.
          When they have paid for the ruin
          of Helen, whom Paris carried away,
          they will never again be so bold as to ravish
          well-born wives out of Greece.
          All these good things I can win by dying.
          Because of me, Greece   1860
          will be free, and my name will be blessed there.
          I must not cling to life too dearly.
          You brought me into the world for the sake
          of everyone in my country,
          and not just for your own.
          Thousands of men have slung shield on shoulder,
                                                 thousands
          have taken hold of the oars
          when they saw their country wronged.   870

And each of them will strike and, if need be, die
for Greece. And shall my one life
stand in the way of it all?
What justice would there be in that? What answer
could I make to those who are ready to die?
There is another thing. It would not
be right for this man
to join battle with the whole of the army
and die for the sake of a woman.
If it means that one man can see the sunlight   1880
what are the lives of thousands of women
in the balance? And if Artemis
demands the offering of my body,
I am a mortal: who am I
to oppose the goddess? It is not to be
considered. I give my life to Greece.
Take me, kill me,
and bring down Troy. That will be my monument
for ages to come. That will be my wedding,
my children, the meaning of my life.   1890
Mother, it is the Greeks
who must rule the barbarians,
not the barbarians the Greeks.
They are born to be slaves; we
to be free.

CHORUS Young woman, what you have said is noble.
It is the role of destiny, in this,
and the role of the goddess,
that are sick.

ACHILLES Daughter of Agamemnon, if I could win you   1900
for my wife, it would prove that some god
wanted to make me happy. I envy
Greece because you are hers, and you
because she is yours. What you have said
is beautiful, and worthy
of your country. You are no match

for the gods, and you have given up
the struggle against them. You have reconciled
what should be with what must be.
But as for me, the more clearly I see your spirit   1910
the more I long to have
so noble a woman for my bride. Look. I want
to save you. To take you home with me.
I call Thetis my mother to witness: now more
than anything it would grieve me
not to pit myself against all the Danaans
and save you.
Think. Death is awesome. Something terrible.

IPHIGENEIA I say what I am about to say
with no regard for anyone.   1920
Tyndareos' daughter,
Helen, will bring on enough fighting, enough
death, for the sake of her body. As for you, stranger,
do not die for me,
and do not kill.
Let me save Greece if that is what I can do.

ACHILLES Oh noble spirit! After that
what is there for me to say? You have chosen.
A splendor in your soul has led you—
why should a man not say it?   1930
But later you may think differently. I want you
to know how I keep my word. I will have these arms
lying by the altar, ready
not to join in your death but to prevent it.
Even when the knife is almost at your neck
it will not be too late to accept my offer.
Turn, and I will not let you die
because of a moment's recklessness.
I will go now to the goddess's temple, with these arms,
and wait there until you come.   1940

ACHILLES *goes off, left, followed by his armor-bearers.*

IPHIGENEIA You are silent. But the tears keep falling.
Mother, why these tears for me?

CLYTEMNESTRA I have reason enough, with this ache in my heart.

IPHIGENEIA No more of that. Do not take
my own courage from me.
Will you do one thing for me?

CLYTEMNESTRA Speak. How could I fail you in anything, child?

IPHIGENEIA Do not cut off a lock of your hair
as is done for the dead.
Put on no mourning for me.   1950

CLYTEMNESTRA What do you mean, child? I am losing you . . .

IPHIGENEIA No. I am saved. My name will be your glory.

CLYTEMNESTRA I don't understand. I am not to mourn for you?

IPHIGENEIA No. I shall have no grave.

CLYTEMNESTRA What of that? It is not the grave we mourn,
but the dead.

IPHIGENEIA The altar of the goddess, the daughter of Zeus,
will be my grave. Tears are forbidden there.

CLYTEMNESTRA My daughter, what you say is true.
I will obey you.   1960

IPHIGENEIA For I am blessed by fortune. It was I
who could bring help to Greece.

CLYTEMNESTRA And what shall I say to your sisters?

IPHIGENEIA Do not dress them in mourning either.

CLYTEMNESTRA Have you some message of love to send them?

IPHIGENEIA Say good-bye to them for me. And bring up
Orestes to be a man
for my sake.

CLYTEMNESTRA (*holding* ORESTES *up to* IPHIGENEIA) Put your arms
around him
since you are looking at him for the last time.   1970

IPHIGENEIA (*hugging him*) Dear child, you did what you could
for those you love.

CLYTEMNESTRA Is there something I can do in Argos,
something that would give you pleasure?

IPHIGENEIA Don't hate my father. He is your husband.

CLYTEMNESTRA He will not like the course he must face because of you.

IPHIGENEIA He destroyed me for the sake of Greece
against his will.

CLYTEMNESTRA But he used lies,
low schemes unworthy of Atreus.

IPHIGENEIA Who will lead me to the place   1980
so that they don't need to touch my hair?

CLYTEMNESTRA I will go with you . . .

IPHIGENEIA (*interrupting*) No. That would not be right.

CLYTEMNESTRA . . . holding on to your gown.

IPHIGENEIA Mother, listen to me. It is better for both of us
if you stay here. One of my father's
servants here can lead me to the meadow
where I am to be killed.

An attendant comes forward and takes IPHIGENEIA'S
hand.

CLYTEMNESTRA My child, you are going . . .

IPHIGENEIA And I shall never come back.   1990

CLYTEMNESTRA Leaving your mother.

IPHIGENEIA As you see. Not because I deserve it.

CLYTEMNESTRA Wait. Do not leave me . . .

IPHIGENEIA Now there must be no tears.
          And you, young women,
          join in my hymn to Artemis the virgin,
          and celebrate my fate.
          Let silence
          descend on the army of the Argives.
          Let the basket be brought,   2000
          light the fire of purification,
          bring the barley. Father
          must lead the procession around the altar.
          I am coming bringing salvation for Greece,
          and victory. Lead me.

          The attendant begins to lead IPHIGENEIA *offstage left
          while she sings her triumphant lament.*

          I who will conquer Troy
          and bring down the city of Ilion.
          Set the wreath on my head.
          Bring the purifying waters.
          Around the temple of Artemis, around   2010
          the altar of blessed Artemis,
          in honor of the goddess begin
          the dance. I will wash away
          with my own blood the spell
          that the oracle revealed.

CHORUS   Oh noble and revered mother,
         we may not shed our tears for you.
         The gods are not worshipped that way.

IPHIGENEIA Young women, sing with me now
         glory to Artemis the goddess   2020
         whose temple faces Chalkis
         where the ships wait, and
         the passion for war is burning,
         here in the narrows of Aulis,
         because of me. Oh Pelasgia where I was born,
         Mycenae,
         home!

CHORUS   Are you invoking the city of Perseus
         which the Cyclopes built?

IPHIGENEIA You brought me up   2030
         to be the light of Greece.
         Dying, I can say it.

CHORUS   Your glory will not die.

IPHIGENEIA Oh light that brings the day, splendor
         of Zeus, I am going
         from this world to another destiny,
         another home. Good-bye
         light that I love.

                    She goes out left, singing. CLYTEMNESTRA *carries*
                         ORESTES *inside the left door of the tent.*

CHORUS   See, she is going. She who will conquer
         Troy and bring down the city of Ilion.   2040
         She leans her head for the victim's garland,
         for the sacred water. She goes
         to drench with her blood the altar
         of the divine goddess,

91

to the sword that will cut
her lovely throat. Your father is waiting
with the pure libations, and the Achaians
are waiting to sail to Troy.
But let us raise our voices to Artemis, daughter
of Zeus, to ask   2050
for a happy destiny. Awesome goddess,
pleased by this human sacrifice, send now
to Phrygia, to the land of deceitful Troy,
the armies of Greece.
There let Agamemnon
wreathe the Achaian weapons with garlands
of victory, and himself win
a crown of unfading glory.

MESSENGER   (enters left and calls at the left door) Daughter of
                        Tyndareos, Clytemnestra,
              come out and hear my message.   2060

CLYTEMNESTRA   (enters, carrying ORESTES) I heard your voice.
                        Here I am,
              distraught, shaking with terror,
              for fear that you have brought some new disaster
              to add to the grief I have.

MESSENGER   It is about your daughter. I have
              something miraculous to tell.

CLYTEMNESTRA   Tell me, tell me at once.

MESSENGER   Beloved mistress, you shall hear everything
                        as it happened, from the beginning,
              unless the seething of my mind   2070
              confuses my words. When we had come to the grove
              sacred to the daughter of Zeus,
              and the flowered meadow of Artemis,
              leading your child
              to the place where the army

92

was ordered to assemble,
the Argives ran, all crowding to the spot.
And King Agamemnon, when he saw his daughter
coming through the grove to the place of sacrifice,
groaned aloud and turned his head, hiding   2080
his eyes and their tears with his robe.
But she came up to her father and said, "Father,
here I am. And I give my body
willingly as a sacrifice
for my country, for all of Greece.
Lead me to the altar
if this is what destiny has decreed.
For my part, I hope
it turns out well for all of you.
May the spoils of victory be yours,   2090
and then the sight of your homes again.
Let none of the Argives lay hands on me.
I will offer my neck in silence,
I will not flinch." That is what she said,
and everyone who heard marvelled
at the girl's bravery and nobility.
Then the herald Talthybios, whose office it was,
called out from among them, to the army,
for the sacred silence,
and the prophet Kalchas drew from its sheath   2100
the whetted knife, and laid it
in the basket worked with gold,
and set the crown upon her head. And Peleus' son
took the basket and the lustral water
and circled the altar, calling out,
"Daughter of Zeus, who bring death
to the wild creatures, who turn
your gleaming star through the darkness, accept
this sacrifice offered to you by us, the army
of the Achaians, and King Agamemnon,   2110
this pure blood
from the throat of a beautiful girl. Now let our
war fleet embark on a smooth voyage

and our weapons bring down the walls of Troy."
Then the sons of Atreus and the whole army stood
with their eyes fixed on the ground, and the priest
took up the knife,
praying, and looked for the place
to plunge it. Pain welled up in me
at that, and I dropped my eyes.   2120
And the miracle happened. Everyone
distinctly heard the sound of the knife
striking, but no one could see
the girl. She had vanished.
The priest cried out, and the whole army
echoed him, seeing
what some god had sent, a thing
nobody could have prophesied. There it was,
we could see it, but we could scarcely
believe it: a deer   2130
lay there gasping, a large
beautiful animal, and its blood ran
streaming over the altar of the goddess.
Then Kalchas, with
such joy as you can imagine, shouted, "Commanders
of the assembled armies of Greece, look:
the goddess has placed this victim
on her altar, a deer from the mountains,
and she accepts this instead of the girl,
rather than stain her altar with noble blood.   2140
With this she is happy, and now she blesses
our voyage to attack Ilion.
Therefore let everyone who is to sail
take heart and go down to his ship,
for today we must leave the hollow gulf of Aulis,
and cross the Aegean Sea."
Then when Hephaistos' flame had left nothing
of the victim but ashes, he offered
the customary prayer for the army's safe return.
Agamemnon sent me to say this,   2150
to tell you of this

destiny which the gods have sent
and of the glory which he has won
among the Greeks. I saw it myself. I was there.
It is plain that your daughter
has been taken up into heaven.
Let this quiet your grief
and put an end to your anger against your husband.
No man living can tell what the gods will do,
but they save those whom they love.   2160
This same day has seen
your daughter dead and brought to life again.

CHORUS With what joy for your sake
        I hear the messenger's words! Showing
        how the girl is alive in heaven with the gods.

CLYTEMNESTRA Oh child, what deity has carried you off?
        How may I address you? How can I be sure,
        how can I know,
        that this is not all a lie, made up
        to silence my bitter grieving?   2170

CHORUS Here comes King Agamemnon. He will tell you
        the same thing.

        AGAMEMNON *enters left, attended by generals, priests
        with the paraphernalia of sacrifice, soldiers, camp-
        followers, sailors, and others taking part in the expedi-
        tion to Troy.*

AGAMEMNON Lady, as for your daughter,
        we have reason to be happy. For truly
        she has the gods for company.
        Now you must take this young calf here
                (*indicates* ORESTES)
        and travel home. The army is preparing to sail.
        Good-bye. My greetings will be slow
        in reaching you from Troy. May you be happy.

CHORUS Son of Atreus, sail   2160
with a light heart to the land of Phrygia,
and return with a light heart
and heavy spoils
from Troy.

AGAMEMNON, *generals, etc., go off left, followed by the*
CHORUS. CLYTEMNESTRA, *carrying* ORESTES, *goes in the*
main door of the tent. She does not look back.

103 *stung by his fate . . .* Editors are wrong to be suspicious of Agamemnon's use of the word *morōi* to mean "fate" here rather than "death." Cf. Homer, *Odyssey* 1.34,35; Aeschylus, *Agamemnon* 1146.

151 *Tell me the rest* Editors sometimes rearrange the order of the lines in the MSS. in order to make the Old Man's speech precede the entire letter; but this is incorrect, as Gilbert Murray saw. Even now that Agamemnon has admitted that to sacrifice Iphigeneia would be a horrible wrong, he is uncertain about his decision to send the letter and pauses while reading it.

190-1 *Mycenae/where the Cyclopes built the walls* In Euripides' day, as in modern times, the walls of Mycenae and Tiryns were remarkable for being built of huge boulders in the style of the long-past Mycenaean age. Such stonework was popularly ascribed to a race of giants, the one-eyed Cyclopes. Euripides repeatedly calls attention to this feature of Agamemnon's capital city (296, 717, 2029), probably to suggest the fundamental cruelty and barbarism of the principles by which its people live. We will not be wrong to think of the savage Cyclopes of Homer's *Odyssey*. See note on 2028-9.

205 *I have crossed the narrows . . .* This choral song is suggestive of Homer's famous Catalogue of Ships from which most of its names and many of its details are taken. The ostensible point is the splendor and magnitude of the host and the greatness of its under-

taking. By his arrangement and selection of detail, however, Euripides exposes this effect to ironic contemplation.

208-10 *Chalkis . . . where the spring/of Arethousa wells up and runs flashing/ down to the sea* This somewhat gratuitous mention of Chalkis' fountain seems intended to remind an Athenian audience of the much more famous fountain of Arethousa on the island of Ortygia in the harbor of Syracuse. It was there that Athenian sea power some seven years previously had received the blow which caused Athens to lose the Peloponnesian War. The parallel between the Athenians' attempt on Syracuse and the Greeks' attempt on Troy is not to be missed.

235-7 *the two that are named Aias . . . Oïleus' son and that son of Telamon/ who is the hope of Salamis . . .* Aias son of Oïleus at the sack of Troy raped Kassandra in Athene's temple. For this crime the goddess brought storm and shipwreck upon the Achaians on their homeward way and Aias himself was drowned.

Aias son of Telamon, the famous bearer of the seven-oxhide shield, also failed to return home. When the arms of Achilles, which had been offered as the prize for being the most effective fighter at Troy, were awarded to Odysseus rather than to Aias, he set out to kill the Greek generals in the night. Athene balked him of his revenge by driving him mad, so that he vented his rage on captured cattle instead. When he came to his senses he killed himself from disappointment and chagrin. The name Aias was associated by Sophocles and others with the cry of grief *aiai*.

238 *and with them Protesilaos . . .* Protesilaos was the first Greek to set foot on the beach at Troy. He was instantly killed, "leaving behind," Homer says, "in Phylake his wife with nail-scored cheeks, and his house half-built." *Iliad* 2.698-702.

239 *Palamedes, child of Poseidon's son . . .* In revenge for Odysseus' treacherous murder of Palamedes at Troy, Poseidon's son Nauplios set false beacons on the rocks of Euboia's Cape Kaphareus and wrecked many of the Greeks on their way home.

242 *Diomedes . . .* In the fighting at Troy, Diomedes wounded both the goddess Aphrodite and the god Ares. Together with Odysseus he

stole the statue of Athene from her temple inside the city. Although he survived the war, he returned home to find his wife unfaithful and his kingdom usurped. He ended his days in Italy after founding one or more cities there.

244 *scion of Ares* . . . an honorific epithet for a warrior, rather than a genealogical statement.

258 *Eumelos, the grandson of Pheres* . . . Eumelos' father Admetos had the honor of having Apollo for his herdsman when that god was expiating his murder of the Cyclopes. Naturally the horses here being driven by Eumelos turned out well, since Apollo raised them. There was a less happy result of Apollo's visit, however. In his gratitude for Admetos' kind treatment, Apollo tricked the Fates into allowing Admetos to survive his appointed death-day, provided he could get some one else to die in his place. As Euripides presents the story in his play *Alcestis*, Admetos was not slow to ask that either his father or his mother take his place in Hades' house. To his chagrin both refused him. He then applied to his wife, Alcestis, who proved more generous, but her consent turned out much worse than his parents' rebuff. After she died he realized that he would have done much better to die himself. As he puts it (*Alcestis* 937-40), "Sorrow will never come to her again. She died in glory, freed from all life's trouble. But I, who should not now be living, have missed my chance to die. I shall lead a life of misery. I see it now."

Partly from grief and partly because she had a right to ask these things, since she was giving her life for his, he swore to her on her deathbed that he would mourn for her perpetually and never take another woman into his house. This left him very little life at all, particularly since he had already disowned his parents for what he regarded as their selfish cruelty towards himself. At the end of the play his friend Herakles brings Alcestis back to him from the dead, but the grisly joke of it is that he makes him accept her before he knows who she is. In doing so Admetos breaks his promise to Alcestis on the same day that he made it, with the result that whatever respect he may still deserve from us after he has showed his willingness to let his wife die for him, lies in ruins. That he is not named here in the normal way as Eumelos' father suggests his disgrace. As alluded to here in our play, however lightly, the story of Admetos is obviously relevant both to Agamemnon's refusal to sacrifice himself for his daughter and to Iphigeneia's willingness to sacrifice herself for him, for Achilles, and for the rest of the Greeks.

279-80 *the son/of Theseus . . .* It is not known whether Akamas or Demophon is meant. In Homer the leader of the Athenians is Menestheus, no relation to Theseus.

286-8 *Kadmos/holding a dragon of gold. Leïtos,/born of the earth . . .* Kadmos founded the Boiotian capital city of Thebes in the following manner: killing the dragon which guarded a spring on the city's site, he sowed its teeth in the earth. Armed men sprang up and, at the instigation of Kadmos, fought together. The five survivors became the founders of the leading families of Thebes. "Leïtos, born of the earth" is a member of one of these families. Since the father of the dragon was Ares, all five families were in a manner descended from the god of war, and strife was seldom absent from the early history of the city. Most notably, the un-witting crimes of Oedipus were followed by the feud between his sons who, having first banished their father, killed one another in their insane contention for the throne. This occurred when one brother brought an Argive army against his own city in the expedition known as "the Seven Against Thebes."

290-1 *the son/of Oïleus . . .* Aias the Less, see note on 235-7.

350-2 *Do you think I am afraid/to look you in the eye, Menelaos?/I am a son of Atreus* By a plausible etymology "Atreus" may be taken to mean "The Unflinching."

531-2 *the same god/who drove you out of your senses* Aphrodite, see 481-6, 1084, 1697-1700.

620-1 *Pelops, whom our father/called "Father" . . .* Pelops, who gave his name to the Peloponnesos, was commonly thought of as the originator of the curse on the house of Atreus because of the violence and trickery with which he won his bride, Hippodameia. Her father, Oinomaos of Olympia, used to test her suitors' worthiness by letting them take her off with them in their chariots and then setting out in pursuit in his. When he caught them, as he invariably did, he speared the young man from behind. Pelops bribed

Oinomaos' charioteer to pull out Oinomaos' linchpin and re-
place it with a wax dummy. Oinomaos was killed in the resulting
wreck, whereupon Pelops, instead of paying off the charioteer,
broke his oath and pushed him off a cliff into the sea. The tricki-
ness of the Peloponnesian nobles is kept in view throughout the
play (e.g. 85-6, 372-4, 620-5, 686, 1012-14, 1978-9, 2053 "deceitful
Troy" after all this!, 2167-9, and see the note on 663).

658-9 *At every step I've tried to see/the right way to act*   We have given Menelaos the benefit of the doubt here, but in Greek his words ex-
press an unmistakable ambiguity. They mean, "I have always
cultivated the best people," just as clearly as they do what we
have translated, and Menelaos has just pointed out that Agamemnon is a more valuable connection than Helen.

663 *Tantalos himself, the son of Zeus . . .*   The respect which the Chorus shows
for the house of Tantalos creates great ironic tension. Tantalos
tried to deceive the gods by serving them the flesh of his son
Pelops at a banquet. The gods detected the ruse and restored
Pelops to life. Altogether, the Atreïds had a bad record where
their children were concerned. Pelops' son Atreus in anger at his
brother Thyestes killed his own nephews and at a feast of pretended reconciliation fed them to their unsuspecting father. If
the line of Tantalos is representative, the great families of
Greece, so envied in this play, are families of monsters.

698-9 *There's no reason for Odysseus/to do anything to injure you or me*   Odysseus' name is explained in the *Odyssey* as meaning "man of hos-
tility," so that actually he is an injurer by nature.

767 *Phrygian pipes . . .*   Mount Ida was in Phrygia; hence Paris' music was com-
posed in the Phrygian mode. Euripides' contemporaries consid-
ered "music," by which they meant both what we call music
and the words set to it, to be half of education. It was thought
to train the soul as "gymnastic" (the other half) trained the
body. The Chorus implies that so much music in the Phrygian
mode had corrupted Paris' character.

1006 *the goddess who reigns in Argos*   Hera, queen of the Olympian divinities.
Her temple near Mycenae was one of the oldest and most
famous in Greece; in fact she was for the Argives what Athene

was for the Athenians. As Zeus' consort she was in particular
goddess of the rights of wives and mothers.

1020-1 *A wise man supports in his house/a good and faithful wife. Or no wife at all*
Distaste for his task makes Agamemnon think of its ultimate
cause. He holds that wives like Helen are not worth room and
board.

1041-2 *the Dioskouroi,/who are stars in heaven* They were identified with the
constellation Gemini and brought safety to sailors at sea, often
appearing as the static-electrical phenomenon known as St.
Elmo's fire.

1050 *Priam's head hewn from its shoulders . . .* In its present incomplete state
the text does not tell us who it is that is beheaded, but compare
Virgil, Aeneid 2.554-8.

1066-7 *the swan with the sinuous neck, whose wings/hid Zeus from Leda . . .*
Zeus was said to have visited Leda in the form of a swan when
he engendered Helen and the Dioskouroi.

1110 *Brief and to the point* The people of Laconia (Sparta) were notoriously
"laconic."

1155-6 *Whose slave? Not mine, certainly, here/among Agamemnon's possessions*
Ironic reference is made to Agamemnon's later appropriation of
Achilles' slave-girl Briseïs, the cause of the "Wrath of Achilles"
which became the subject of Homer's *Iliad*.

1501 *Here she is, obedient to your command* Obedience was especially cultivated
among the Spartans, with whom Agamemnon and Clytemnestra
are associated. Cf. 831, 983-4, and the epitaph for the Spartan
dead at Thermopylai. Euripides is treating Spartan virtue with
irony.

1682-3 *a deadly struggle begins/between the sons of Atreus and their children . . .*
Iphigeneia's resistance to being sacrificed by her father is a pre-
monition of her father's death at Clytemnestra's hands, sacrificed, as Clytemnestra will say, to Iphigeneia's Fury. From this
murder, in turn, will spring Orestes' murder of his mother.

1722-3 *oh high slopes of Ida where Priam/once left a baby* . . . Priam's queen
Hecuba dreamed that she gave birth to a burning torch, and the
soothsayers proclaimed that the child with which she was then
pregnant would destroy his city. Priam exposed the baby on Mt.
Ida, but a bear found it and suckled it, and it lived to be brought
up by shepherds. As it grew to manhood so great was the child's
prowess that the shepherds called it Alexandros, which means
"Protector." Alexandros soon found his way to the city of Troy,
where he was recognized as Paris, the prince who had been
exposed.

1833-4 *You mean that will stop them/from killing her?* Reading a question mark
at the end of 1367 in the Greek.

1923-5 *As for you, stranger,/do not die for me,/and do not kill* . . . As it turns
out of course, Achilles will both kill and die because of Iphigeneia, for only if she is sacrificed can the war take place in
which he will both kill many and be killed himself. Iphigeneia's
allowing herself to be slaughtered will cost more lives than resistance would.

1966-8 *And bring up/Orestes to be a man/for my sake* Orestes' "manhood"
turned out to mean that he must kill his mother.

1979 *low schemes unworthy of Atreus* It was Atreus who revenged himself on his
brother Thyestes by murdering Thyestes' children. He then in-
vited him to a banquet and served him his sons' flesh disguised
as game. See note on 663.

1984 *holding on to your gown* Clytemnestra earlier thought that she might save
Iphigeneia's life by this gesture (1832-4), and it certainly seems
an appropriate one, whether or not it will do any good. Nevertheless, Clytemnestra now lets herself be dissuaded from it, as
from those other actions of pathos and protest which are proposed but not performed: Iphigeneia's dramatic supplication of
Achilles (1360-1), and Clytemnestra's passionate search for him
through the camp (1406-7).

2006-7 *I who will conquer Troy/and bring down the city of Ilion* These words,
repeated at 2039-40, allude unmistakably to the striking choral
passage in Aeschylus' *Agamemnon* where it is suggested that

Helen's name spells "death of ships, death of men, death of the city": *helenas, helandros, heleptolis* (689). Iphigeneia has tried to disassociate herself from Helen in every way (1919-26), but by calling herself *heleptolis* here as she leaves the stage she makes us realize that by letting herself be sacrificed she has become as responsible as Helen is for the tragedy of the Trojan War. It is no exaggeration to say that she might better hang herself than incur responsibility for the sack of Troy. Like many another noble and devoted young person in similar circumstances, she has been duped by false patriotism, "and that," to paraphrase Aeschylus' Kassandra in another connection, "is far the saddest thing of all."

2028-9 *the city of Perseus/which the Cyclopes built* . . . By a plausible etymology, Perseus means "he who destroys." There is an obvious clash between this significance and Iphigeneia's belief, expressed three lines below, that the city of Perseus has brought her up to be "the light of Greece." The savagery of the Cyclopes has been remarked in the note on 190-1.

2103-5 *And Peleus' son/took the basket and the lustral water/and circled the altar* . . . Achilles performs the role we have been led to expect that Agamemnon will play (563-6, 2002-3, 2046-7). This is not a forger's clumsy inconsistency, but a masterstroke of irony. We recognize instantly that Achilles' interest in the glory to be won at Troy is even greater than Agamemnon's, and that he has never thought for a moment, in his confidence in the power of destiny in these matters, that he would have to keep his extravagant promises to save Iphigeneia's life (1285ff., 1302ff., 1335ff., 1377ff.).

2108 *your gleaming star* . . . The moon. Artemis, while not exactly the moon-goddess (Selene, whose name means simply "moon," is that), is often associated with it.

2147-8 *nothing/of the victim but ashes* . . . It will be difficult for anyone to determine, after the fact, whether it was an animal or a girl that was sacrificed. Or so a bystander familiar with Pelopid and Spartan chicanery might conclude.

2167-70 *How can I be sure* . . . */that this is not all a lie, made up/to quiet my bitter grieving?* Clytemnestra never became sure. Every member of

Euripides' audience knew how in her anger over Iphigeneia's death she murdered Agamemnon when he returned home from Troy, just as she predicted she would in our play (1586-8).

2171-2 *Here comes King Agamemnon. He will tell you/the same thing* The Chorus by now has come to recognize Agamemnon's way of doing things.

2176 *this young calf here . . .* Agamemnon was prepared to treat Iphigeneia like a calf also. Cf. 1455-67, 1492-4.

2178-9 *My greetings will be slow/in reaching you from Troy* This is probably an ironic allusion to the chain of beacons by which Clytemnestra arranged to hear of Agamemnon's victory, and therefore of his return, almost before he knew of it himself. In this way she had time to prepare his murder.

GLOSSARY

ACHAI'ANS, collective name for the Greeks.

ACHIL'LES, the greatest hero of the Greeks.

AGAME'MNON, king of Mycenae and supreme leader of the Greeks at Troy.

AI'AKOS, grandfather of Achilles.

AI'AS, the name of two separate heroes, the one son of Oïleus of Lokris, the other of Telamon of Salamis. The Romans spelled this name Aiax, and so it became "Ajax" in English literary tradition.

AIGI'NA, nymph, daughter of the river-god Asopos, gave her name to the island in the Saronic Gulf off Attica. Great-grandmother of Achilles.

AI'NIAN, from the district of Ainis in north-central Greece.

ALEXAN'DROS, or ALEXAN'DER, name given to Paris when he was brought up unrecognized among the shepherds of Mt. Ida. See note on 1722-3.

ALPHEI'OS, river of the western Peloponnesos.

APHRODI'TE, goddess of love.

API'DANOS, river in Thessaly.

A'RES, god of war.

ARETHOU'SA, name of a spring at Chalkis.

AR'GIVES, collective name for the Greeks. In Homer "Argos" in its extended sense can mean all of Greece.

AR'GOS, city near Mycenae but more often used in an extended sense to mean (1) the district in which both were situ-

ated, or (2) Agamemnon's domain in general, the whole
of Greece.

AR'TEMIS, goddess of untamed womanhood, of wild animals, and
of the young of all creatures, especially human beings.
Hence goddess of childbirth and its mysteries.

ASO'POS, a river-god.

A'TREUS, king of Mycenae, son of Pelops and father of Agamemnon and Menelaos.

AT'TICA, country in which Athens is situated.

AU'LIS, site of a temple of Artemis on the coast of Boiotia, across
the Euripos straits from the city of Chalkis on the island
of Euboia.

BAK'CHOS, another name for Dionysos, god of ecstasy and wine.

BOIO'TIA, country north of Attica in Greece.

CHAL'KIS, city on the island of Euboia.

CHEI'RON, a centaur (half man, half horse). He lived in a cave
on Mt. Pelion and was tutor to many Greek heroes.

CLYTEMNE'STRA, wife of Agamemnon.

CYCLO'PES, a race of giants characterized by having only one eye,
located in the center of their foreheads.

CY'PRIAN, the Cyprian goddess Aphrodite, supposed to be con-
nected with the island of Cyprus.

CY'PRIS, Aphrodite, the Cyprian goddess.

DANA'ANS, collective term for the Greeks. Danaos was an early
settler at Argos.

DAR'DANOS, son of Zeus and founder of the Trojan royal line.

DIOME'DES, of Argos, Greek hero at Troy.

DIOS'KOUROI, "sons (kouroi) of Zeus (Dios)," Kastor and Poly-
deukes, offspring of Zeus' encounter with Leda.

ECHI'NAI, also called Echinades, islands off the mouth of the
Gulf of Corinth, to the north.

E'LIS, city-state in western Peloponnesos.

EPEI'ANS, a Greek tribe in the district of Elis.

E'ROS, god of sexual desire.

EUBOI'A, a large and long island across from Aulis on the north-
eastern shore of the Greek mainland.

EUME'LOS, son of Admetos son of Pheres; according to Homer

his horses were the most beautiful of all the Greeks' at Troy, next to Achilles'.

EURI'POS, famous narrows between Aulis in Boiotia and the city of Chalkis on the island of Euboia.

EURO'TAS, the river on which Sparta is situated.

EU'RYTOS, leader of the Epeians.

GA'NYMEDE, son of Dardanos of Troy. Smitten with his beauty, Zeus took the form of an eagle and carried him off from his father's pastures to Olympos, the home of the gods.

GERE'NIAN, from the city of Gerenon in Messenia. Nestor was visiting there when Herakles killed his father and all his brothers at their home in Pylos.

GOU'NEUS, king of the Ainians. He is mentioned but once in Homer—in the Catalogue of Ships.

HA'DES, "The Unseen," god of the underworld.

HE'LEN, daughter of Leda and Tyndareos, thought by many to have been fathered by Zeus in the shape of a swan.

HEPHAI'STOS, god of fire and metal-working.

HE'RA, supreme goddess on Olympos, sister and consort of Zeus.

HER'MES, god of flocks and herds, travelers, business, and heralds.

HERMI'ONE, daughter of Helen and Menelaos.

I'DA, mountain near Troy.

I'LION, name of the citadel at Troy.

I'NACHOS, river-god, king, and ancestor of the people of Argos.

IPHIGENEI'A, daughter of Agamemnon and Clytemnestra.

KA'DMOS, founder and first king of Thebes in Boiotia.

KAL'CHAS, soothsayer for the Greek army.

KA'PANEUS, father of Sthenelos. He was perhaps the most hubristic of the hubristic "Seven Against Thebes."

KASSAN'DRA, daughter of Priam and Hecuba. The god Apollo, being in love with her, gave her the power of prophecy.

LAËR'TES, father of Odysseus.

LE'DA, mother of Helen and Clytemnestra.

LE'ITOS, of Thebes, descended from the dragon's teeth, commander of the Boiotians.

LO'KRIS, country in northern Greece.

LY'DIAN, from Lydia, a country near Troy allied with the Trojans.

ME'GES, leader of the Taphians. He is a fighter of some prominence in the Iliad.

MEKI'STEUS, son of Talaos and father of Euryalos the leader of the contingent from Argos in the narrower sense (see "Argos").

MENELA'OS, brother of Agamemnon and husband of Helen of Troy.

MERI'ONES, leader of the Cretans in the Greek army at Troy.

MYCE'NAE, city dominating the Argive plain at the head of the Argolic gulf in eastern Peloponnesos.

MYR'MIDONS, subjects of Peleus and Achilles.

NE'REÏDS, sea-nymphs, daughters of Nereus, a sea-god and "Old Man of the Sea." Achilles' mother Thetis was a Nereïd.

NE'REUS, a sea-god.

NE'STOR, elder statesman and leader of the Greeks at Troy.

NI'REUS, named by Homer as the handsomest of the Achaians at Troy, next to Achilles.

ODYS'SEUS, Greek leader, a master of stratagems.

OÏ'LEUS, of Lokris, father of the lesser Aias.

OINO'NE, ancient name of the island of Aigina.

OLYM'POS, a mythical singer.

ORE'STES, only son of Agamemnon and Clytemnestra.

OR'PHEUS, a legendary musician. The power of his music would have served even to bring back his wife Eurydice from the dead, if he had not looked back to see whether she was following.

PALAME'DES, son of Nauplios son of Poseidon, Greek hero at Troy. He was said to have invented the game of checkers.

PAL'LAS ATHE'NE, companion of heroes, goddess of proficiency and success.

PA'RIS, son of Priam king of Troy.

PELAS'GIA, ancient name for Argos.

PE'LEUS, father of Achilles.

PE'LION, mountain on the Magnesian Peninsula in Thessaly,

southernmost of the chain which it forms with Mts. Olympos and Ossa.

PE'LOPS, first of the Atreïd line in Peloponnesus.

PER'GAMOS, like "Ilion," a name for the citadel of Troy.

PER'SEUS, the famous Greek hero who, among other adventures, cut off the Gorgon's head and turned people to stone with it. He was grandson, by Danaë, of Akrisios, king of "Argos," which as we have seen may include Mycenae.

PHARSA'LIA, city of Thessaly.

PHE'RES, father of Admetos whose son Eumelos was one of the Greeks at Troy. Pheres is best remembered for his refusal to give his life in exchange for his son's.

PHOI'BE, sister of Helen and Clytemnestra, daughter of Leda and Tyndareos.

PHRY'GIA, country in northwest Asia Minor in which Troy was situated.

PHTHI'A, district in Thessaly in northern Greece.

PHY'LEUS, father of Meges who leads the Taphians.

PLEI'ADES, constellation of seven stars, conceived of as either the seven daughters of the giant Atlas or as a flock of seven doves (peleiai or peleiades). In either case they were appropriately pursued by the hunter Orion.

POSEI'DON, god of the waters and the earthquake.

PRI'AM, king of Troy.

PROTESILA'OS, a Greek hero, member of the expedition to Troy.

PY'LOS, Nestor's capital city, situated in Messenia in western Peloponnesos.

SA'LAMIS, island in the Saronic Gulf, near Athens.

SI'MOÏS, river at Troy.

SI'PYLOS, mountain on the frontier between Lydia and the Greek cities of the Asia Minor coast.

SI'RIUS, the Dog-star, who, together with the constellation of the hunter Orion, pursues the Pleiades through the sky at night.

SI'SYPHOS, king of Corinth and a great rogue and trickster who outwitted Death himself. Those who wished to speak ill of Odysseus claimed that his real father was not Laërtes but Sisyphos.

SPAR'TA, chief city of Lacedaemon, the country occupying the Eurotas valley in south-central Peloponnesos.

STHE'NELOS, a leader of the Argives, companion of Diomedes.

TA'LAOS, father of Mekisteus.

TAN'TALOS, son of Zeus and father of Pelops. He was the first of the Atreïd line. Another Tantalos, son of Thyestes, was said by some to have been Clytemnestra's first husband, murdered by Agamemnon.

TALTHY'BIOS, herald of the Greek army.

TA'PHIAN, belonging to a piratical race living in the Echinades islands, north of the mouth of the Gulf of Corinth.

TE'LAMON, of Salamis, father of the greater Aias.

THE'SEUS, the greatest king of Athens.

THE'STIOS, of Aetolia, father of Leda.

THE'TIS, sea-nymph, mother of Achilles.

THRO'NION, city in Lokris, about ten miles east of Thermopylai.

TROY, great city of "barbarian" (i.e. non-Greek) Asia Minor, modern Turkey.

TYNDA'REOS, king of Sparta and husband of Leda, mother of Helen and Clytemnestra.

ZEUS, sky-god, "father of gods and men," ruler of the world.

CPSIA information can be obtained at www.ICGtesting.com
Printed in the USA
BVOW02s1150120814

362533BV00001B/2/P